Sustainable Communities
David J. Wellman

 World Council of Churches . New York . Geneva

Sustainable Communities

World Council of Churches
475 Riverside Drive, Rm. 915
New York, NY 10115, United States

World Council of Churches
150 route de Ferney, P. O. Box 2100
1211 Geneva 2, Switzerland

Excerpts from *Risks of Faith* (Boston: Beacon Press, 1999), Copyright © 1999 by James H. Cone, reprinted with permission of the author.
From *Earth Community, Earth Ethics* (Maryknoll, NY: Orbis Books, 1996), Copyright © 1996 Larry Rasmussen, reprinted with permission of the author.
From *The Zapatista Social Netwar in Mexico* (Santa Monica, CA: The RAND Corporation, 1998), Copyright © 1998 David Ronfeldt, John Arquilla, Graham E. Fuller and Melissa Fuller, reprinted with permission from the RAND Corporation

ISBN 0-9715757-0-3

Library of Congress Control Number (LCCN) 2001097189

Printed in the United States by Kutztown Publishing Co., Kutztown, PA

Edited by Vivian Harrower, Toronto, Canada

Cover Design and Illustration by Michelle Wells

Table of Contents

Acknowledgements

This project is the product of an extraordinary community of people who continue to support me in my work. I owe a special debt of gratitude to my advisor Larry Rasmussen, who has been for me the kind of teacher I can only hope to be. I am also deeply indebted to my other mentor at Union Theological Seminary, Beverly Harrison, for her extraordinary wisdom and generosity. I would also like to thank Martin Robra from the World Council, for his creative insight, enthusiasm and encouragement. While there are many of my fellow students to whom I owe thanks, there are none whose counsel and friendship I value more than Lisa Anderson's. Among Union's students, I would also like to thank Mary Foulke, who introduced me to the work of white anti-racism groups, and changed my perspective forever.

I reserve the greatest thanks for my family, who make almost everything possible: my father Norbert, my mother Ann and my sister Kaie. I wish to also thank my in-laws, the Robinsons: especially Jack, Judy and Chris. Finally, I want to thank my life partner, Andy Robinson; his love and patience have taught me that there are far more important things than writing papers. Together, the Wellmans and the Robinsons have profoundly re-defined my working understanding of the terms "community" and "family". Their example of love is the best education I have ever received.

This is dedicated to Dorothy Del Ridings, my grandmother, who taught me how to read, and how to plant a vegetable garden.

David Wellman
New York, February 2001

Introduction:
Come, Holy Spirit

With increasing clarity, it has become apparent that the Earth's carrying capacity is being overwhelmed by the demands of its human occupants. While some have clearly contributed much more to Earth's distress than others, the ultimate conclusion remains the same: we are now collectively confronting the destructive results of long held systems, beliefs and practices which can no longer be sustained. In the midst of such a crisis, perhaps the most discouraging fact of all lies in the popular belief that forces beyond anyone's control have placed the human community (and Earth itself) on an unalterable course. Whether through statements invoking the primacy of the market or simply non-negotiable human instinct, many in the human community have been encouraged to limit their desire for change to their own lives or those of their closest allies. Regretfully, such isolated struggles often do not come close to touching the core of what made them necessary in the first place

The search for sustainability presents multiple challenges that cannot be addressed in isolation. Breaking with the past while simultaneously establishing new ways of living as human communities will by necessity become the order of the day. Such an undertaking will therefore require directly confronting those forces, traditions, beliefs and habits which lie at the heart of unsustainability, and in turn offering a strong and profoundly creative response.

Yet where will the creativity and strength come from to win such a fight? In 1991, the World Council of Churches gathered in Canberra under the theme, "Come, Holy Spirit, Renew the Whole Creation", a title which made central the one who is often (at least in many Northern circles) the least discussed member of the Trinity. Perhaps the time has now come to revisit the theme of Canberra, and to ask ourselves how we intend to be more fully open to the presence of the grace and wisdom of God in the midst of our most worldly struggles. All indications point to the conclusion that fighting for sustainability will require no less than this.

Building sustainability will require human communities to see and to act in a manner which defies many social, cultural, economic and religious conventions, while rejecting models many have thought to be beyond the reach of change. While such foundational changes might appear daunting, they should hardly be seen as impossible. As many in the World Council have affirmed, the market is not

God; God is God. It is only logical, then, that it is God and *all of God's creation* that have the power to determine what can and cannot be changed. Therefore, as a community who claims the companionship of and allegiance to a living and breathing God, let us invoke the Spirit in taking up one of our most profound challenges. Come, Holy Spirit, and *renew the whole Creation*. Come Holy Spirit, and renew our sense of imagination, strength and creativity. Come Holy Spirit, and renew and expand our sense of justice, and thus our willingness to act on the imagination of Jesus. Come, Holy Spirit, you speaker of all languages, and teach us how we can more fully and intelligently communicate across boundaries of difference. Come, Holy Spirit, and guide our actions. Come, Holy Spirit, and be with us now.

BEGINNING THE CONVERSATION

As a student of ethics, I have become convinced that any discussion of an ethic which is to be lived out must place at its centre a clear explanation of its definition of "community". Such a definition should include how the community recognizes its members, what it defines as "accountability", and how it works to ensure its own survival. Ethical claims regarding community often explain more about the agenda of the person, group or movement making them than they actually intend to reveal. For this reason, when I am trying to understand a new thinker or movement, I begin by asking them to help me answer these questions: What is their definition of community? What do they believe is central to a community's ability to remain physically, socially, economically, politically and spiritually sustainable? How inclusive is their definition of community? Is their understanding of the integrity of the human community linked to the integrity of the greater non-human community?

As conversations regarding environmental ethics have evolved, working definitions of the terms "community", "sustainability" and "development" have come to be expanded, redefined, and challenged. In its long-standing engagement with environmental justice issues, the World Council of Churches has endeavoured to find a vocabulary and a strategy which best reflects its own evolving goals and alliances. At the same time, the last three decades have seen the World Council working closely with a variety of environmentally-focused secular and religious movements, which often used divergent vocabulary while claiming a common goal.

something more. With this in mind, this project is also an effort to engage issues of strategy and action, in an attempt to examine how the sentiments of our emerging vocabularies might be physically put into play. To this end, this project seeks to invite readers into a conversation regarding how the suggestions, strategies and tactics for building and preserving sustainability described in these pages might be translated into a form which is useful in one's own particular context.

The chapters are arranged as follows. Chapter 1 provides an overview of some of the theological themes which have guided the WCC in approaching the sustainable development debate. Chapter 2 offers a synthesis of the Council's definitions of "sustainable", "sustainability" and "development", in an attempt to provide a working WCC definition of "sustainable development". This chapter then moves to examining questions of strategy regarding the Council's engagements with secular actors and organizations within the sustainable development debate. Chapter 3 presents the work of two thinkers, Larry Rasmussen and James Cone, as a foundation for pushing our understanding of the concept of sustainable communities to a deeper level. Chapter 4 gives an overview of some of the major themes, observations and critiques contained in WCC documents on the subject of building sustainability within the reality of a globalized economy. Chapter 5 describes and analyzes the tactics one community used to defend itself from forces who favoured their "development" and some of the lessons which can be drawn from their experience. The chapter concludes with a reflection on the challenge of inclusivity and solidarity in the struggle to build sustainable communities. Finally, chapter 5 is followed by appendices which include eleven World Council documents. Written by some of the most influential participants in the Council's work on sustainability, community and ethics, these selections have been chosen to offer the reader a broader perspective on the Council's ongoing work. The voices which emerge from these documents help to illustrate the historical progression of the Council's positions on sustainable communities, as well as offer insights into the work which lies ahead.

It would be dishonest to imply through silence that this project was somehow written by an objective observer. I am a white man who carries a United States passport and who enjoys considerable economic privilege. For this reason, the reader should liberally apply what one of my teachers calls the "hermeneutic of suspicion" to the following pages.[4] With that in mind, I offer this writing as simply one particular interpreter of ideas, who is in need of many further conversations and many more conversation partners.

[1]This placement of WCC activities in relation to world events is taken from a presentation made by David Hallman at the World Council's 1998 General Assembly in Harare, Zimbabwe.
[2]Gnanadason, Aruna, from her preface to James Martin-Schramm's *Population Perils and the Churches' Response* (Geneva: WCC Publications, 1997), p. x.
[3]Recent discussions at the JPC Consultation at Union Theological Seminary, New York (December 15-16, 2000) pushed this discussion further. Beyond the problematic implications of speaking of one singular "community", participants noted that the word "sustainable" also holds a number of possible negative connotations. They observed that the term "sustainable communities" somehow implied qualities which were static rather than dynamic. Participants also stated that some forms of community, which are grounded in structural injustice, should not in fact be sustained. Alternatives were suggested which could replace "sustainable", such as "life-giving", "life-affirming" or "viable". In the place of "sustainability", participants to the Consultation suggested the use of the word "viability" or the phrase "life-giving practices". Participants observed that such words or phrases were better suited to conveying new local-global dynamics, affirmations of diversity, and acceptance of the reality of conflict. Along with such specifics, the discussions taking place at the Consultation pointed out a more far-reaching truth: namely that all terms used in the eco-theology/sustainability/justice debates carry specific limitations, whether they are used in their own contexts or in international efforts to universalize their use. The readers of this text are therefore encouraged to join in the ongoing discussions regarding which terms are best suited to the work of building what some currently refer to as "sustainable communities".
[4]I am deeply indebted to Beverly Harrison, my mentor and friend, for introducing me to this most useful term. The term, *hermeneutics of suspicion* was first used in the context of theology by Juan Luis Segundo, in his book *The Liberation of Theology* (Maryknoll, NY: Orbis, 1976).

I
APPROACHING SUSTAINABLE DEVELOPMENT: SELECTED THEOLOGICAL STATEMENTS FROM THE WORLD COUNCIL OF CHURCHES, 1991-1994

Through its long-standing involvement in ecological and economic concerns, the World Council of Churches has gone on record as a strong advocate of policies favouring environmental and economic reforms. From as early as 1974 in Bucharest,[1] through the most recent Visser 't Hooft Consultation at Bossey, the WCC has used the word "sustainable" in describing its vision of a new form of human cooperation and community.[2] The word "development" has also played a long-standing and important role in the vocabulary of the WCC, although its use has referred not to the dominant definition (re: economic growth), but rather to community development, and, in certain cases, appropriate technology.[3] Yet while it is important to consider the ways in which the Council has frequently employed the words "sustainable" and "development", it is equally important to observe how infrequently the WCC has been inclined to use the combined term "sustainable development".[4]

Such a choice on the part of the WCC has not prevented it from participating in a variety of events that have liberally employed the concept of sustainable development in their proceedings. In such diverse settings as the UNCED gathering in Rio de Janeiro, the Third Conference of Parties in Kyoto, and the most recent gathering of the UN Commission on Sustainable Development, the WCC has remained in substantive dialogue with numerous groups and individuals who are working on how to better define and implement the principles of sustainable development. Given such a level of involvement, one might ask: What are the principles which guide the World Council at such gatherings? The following represents an attempt to glean from a selected group of WCC writings some of the underlying theological claims which guide the Council's participation in secular environmental conferences.

A wealth of information toward this end can be found in the WCC document entitled *Now is the Time: The Final Document and Other Texts from the World Convocation on Justice, Peace and the Integrity of Creation.*[5] The gathering in Seoul, in March 1990, provided a platform for a diverse array of voices and theological insights regarding, among other topics, the destruction of the ecosphere. The theological statements and claims which emerge from this final document provide at least one route, yet by no means the only one, through which one can begin to discern some of the predispositions the World Council brings into discussions of sustainable development. These predispositions are described with such words as "covenant", "accountability", "solidarity", "affirmation", "resistance" and "hope".

In its "Preamble to Act of Covenanting", *Now is the Time* clearly spells out the World Council's understanding of God, humanity and creation as being intrinsically linked:

> God's covenant extends beyond the present inhabitants of the earth to future generations and to the whole of creation. If humanity is to survive, the rights of future generations and the intrinsic value of nature must be recognized.[6]

Such a holistic view of creation precludes compartmentalizing the ecosphere or giving priority to short-term gains over long-range planning. Further, this statement's valuation of non-human nature is hardly economic. Rather, *Now is the Time* goes on to state

> We <u>affirm</u> that the world, as God's handiwork, has its own inherent integrity; that land, waters, air, forests, mountains and all creatures, including humanity, are "good" in God's sight. The integrity of creation has a social aspect which we recognize as peace with justice, and an ecological aspect which we recognize in the self-renewing, sustainable character of natural ecosystems.[7]

Clearly, the WCC position argues that the commodification of nature goes against the inherent integrity of God's creation. Thus, one can see *Now is the Time* as a document which rejects the notion of a strictly human system being able to determine value. Rather, the ecosphere, inclusive of humanity, is described as intrinsically possessing its own self-sustaining value, as well as the ability to model sustainability for its human inhabitants. Such a non-anthropocentric view of valuation points to an understanding of sustainability which does not emerge from an economic system.

Now is the Time's theological statements regarding the destruction of creation and humanity's role are influenced by an interpretation of scripture which rejects humanity's claim to ownership of the natural world. Instead, the document argues that

> Biblical statements, such as "to have dominion" and "subdue the earth", have been misused through the centuries to justify destructive actions toward the created order. As we repent of this violation, we accept the biblical teaching that people, created in the image of God, have a special responsibility as servants in reflecting God's creating and sustaining love, to care for creation and to live in harmony with it.[8]

Humanity in this light cannot therefore be seen as the invincible "crown of creation", but rather as a group which is defined by its responsibility and interdependence. This responsibility is one which is clearly more focused on the sustainability of greater or inclusive community than that of economic profitability. On this point, the WCC's final JPIC document leaves no doubt as to the ramifications of such a position.

> We will resist the claim that anything in creation is merely a resource for human exploitation. We will resist species extinction for human benefit; consumerism and harmful mass production; pollution of land, air and water; all human activities which are now leading to probable rapid climate change; and policies and plans which contribute to the disintegration of creation.[9]

Clearly, the World Council enters into discussions of sustainable development with a strong predisposition toward rejecting many existing frameworks of analysis, particularly those which begin with addressing the needs of the market over that of greater creation.

In addition to its rejection of those practices which exploit the non-human world, *Now is the Time* draws important links between destructive ecological practices and the injustices the human community perpetrates upon its own most vulnerable members:

> We will resist any policy that treats land merely as a marketable commodity; that allows speculation at the expense of the poor; that dumps poisonous wastes into the land and the waters; that promotes the exploitation, unequal distribution or contamination of the land and its products; and that prevents those who live directly from the land from being its real trustees.[10]

Such a statement is in keeping with the World Council's established inclination toward speaking in terms of "sustainable society".[11] Further, this position reflects a WCC membership which stands on both sides of the North/South split, and is therefore sincerely committed to justice issues which are inclusive of both land and people. It is out of faith and such tandem concerns that *Now is the Time* advocates the power of a radical hope, one which emerges through joining with rather than directing others:

> Christian hope is a resistance movement against fatalism. We want to share this hope with all people. We want to join with them in the same movement. We want to learn from their experience and from the hope by which they are sustained in their struggle.[12]

Given such statements, it is difficult to imagine the World Council being open to the current approach guiding the majority of sustainable development discussions, which assumes the centrality of the market economy and then moves outward toward ecological considerations. Clearly, the WCC's theological claims embrace a different guiding principle, one which cannot be described as patently affirming the expectations of the market.

A second important source of information which documents the eco-theological reflections of the World Council is found in the document entitled *Searching for the New Heavens and the New Earth: An Ecumenical Response to UNCED*.[13] This paper is the product of a WCC-sponsored ecumenical gathering which occurred in Rio de Janeiro during the 1992 conference known as the Earth Summit. *Searching for the New Heavens* is, in effect, the World Council's response to the Earth Summit, though it is hardly the only response the Council has offered.

Searching for the New Heavens reaffirms many of the theological claims and statements expressed in *Now is the Time*, particularly regarding the Council's belief that God's covenant extends to all creatures.[14] What this Rio document expands on, however, is the link between acknowledging such a covenant, and the Christian responsibility to fight for the preservation of biodiversity:

> The richness and variety of life forms on earth bears witness to God's creativity. We acknowledge that the traditional anthropocentric nature of Christian theology has contributed to one species, human beings, destroying and threatening many other life forms. Furthermore, the powerful within the human community are seeking to gain ownership rights over life forms to extract maximum economic profit.[15]

In light of this statement, one is drawn to conclude that the World Council's questioning of the current guiding paradigm of sustainable development is founded on more than one concern. For not only is the World Council expressing its rejection of an economically-centred value system, it is also confessing Christianity's historic and continuing collusion with the dominant market-driven interpretation of development.

In addition to an economic critique, the WCC's statements in *Searching for the New Heavens* sharply call into question the popularly held view of what constitutes humanity's normative role vis-à-vis the ecosphere. For rather than depicting the human standing above creation as its ultimate earthly arbiter, the Council's statements describe humanity as embedded *within* creation. At the same time, this document is quite clear that the normative role of humanity within the ecosphere begins with the acts of listening to and learning from creation:

> Anthropocentric, hierarchical, and patriarchal understandings of creation lead to the alienation of human beings from each other, from nature, and from God. The current ecological crisis calls us to move toward an eco-centered theology of creation which emphasizes God's spirit in creation (Gen. 1:2, Ps. 104), and human beings as an integral part of nature. Instead of dominating nature, men and women have the responsibility to preserve, cultivate the earth, and to work with God for the sustainabilityof the planet.[16]

Therefore, effective human action can only emerge from a community which makes the conscious choice to acknowledge three things: (1) its need for education; (2) its horizontal relationship with other members of creation; and (3) the understanding that one works with, and not on behalf of, God. Sustainability, therefore, takes on not only the material implications of preserving the physical world, it embodies a series of new relationships between members of the human community, between the human and non-human earthly community, and between those who have participated in the destruction of creation and the one who is called the Author of creation.

Another important contribution to the World Council's efforts to express the theological underpinnings of its understanding of sustainability and development is found in the document entitled, *Accelerated Climate Change: Sign of Peril, Test of Faith*.[17] This 1994 paper underscores themes which emerged in the Seoul and Rio documents, while emphasizing even more fully an understanding of God's creation which defies any manner of compartmentalization:

> As Christians we affirm and seek to discern God's action and
> will in the present crisis. In this crisis, compounded in violation
> of intricate natural systems and the disruptive exploitation of
> vulnerable human communities, nature has become co-victim
> with the poor. Earth and people will be liberated to thrive
> together, or not at all.[18]

Such an admonition to those who seek to separate portions of the ecosphere once again exemplifies a theology which reflects the Council's Northern and Southern membership. At the same time, *Accelerated Climate Change* does not gloss over important distinctions which must be drawn regarding the ecosphere's inhabitants:

> The Creator who loves the whole creation calls its human
> oppressors to account for the arrogance, greed, and care-
> lessness that endanger creation's future.[19]

The document is also clear in pointing out that although the human community must confront the results of its actions, it must also "make a distinction between the 'luxury emissions of the rich' and the 'survival emissions of the poor'".[20]

Such observations are congruent with those highlighted in both the Seoul and Rio documents, namely that the ecological crisis is emblematic of the absence of justice, both in inter-human relationships as well as those in greater creation. *Accelerated Climate Change* points out that the call for justice for non-human creation is in keeping with our understanding of scriptural teachings.[21] In the same way, meaningful, sustainable justice for the human community is also scripturally mandated, and impossible to achieve in the absence of fighting for the integrity of the entire ecosphere:

> Reducing the threat of climate change requires fundamental
> changes in the way that people relate to each other and the
> earth. It requires changes that build community. We under-
> stand community in a broad sense. It includes the centrality of
> the local setting in which people together meet their needs
> and find meaning......(It also) encompasses our relationships
> beyond the human family.[22]

One could say that building community is the theological hermeneutic of the World Council's approach to issues of sustainability, and, subsequently, one could argue, development as well. First and foremost among the requirements of such a strategy is recognizing that being and working in community is a desirable end. The second task is realizing that truly sustainable communities are comprised of more than simply human members. While these goals might appear modest, the present scope of the destruction of the ecosphere argues otherwise.

How then can we build the sustainable communities that we are still endeavouring to fully describe? One answer offered by those who drafted *Accelerated Climate Change* argues that

> Only in humility and in openness do we presume to speak of God's action or to project God's purpose for the years and decades immediately ahead. Nevertheless, as a people nurtured by the biblical story that still continues, we dare to believe that God calls us to participate with God in God's own work of stopping the degradation of Earth's protective mantle and engaging in the other tasks of protecting and restoring the creation, human and nonhuman.
>
> With God, in these tasks, we find meaning, joy, and hope. Encountering formidable opposition, we do not know the extent to which our human efforts can reverse injustices, change the economic order, and stem the tide of global warming. Nevertheless, trusting that our efforts can be consistent with God's purposes, even when achievement is not measurable, we may eagerly accept God's invitation to adventurous faithfulness.[23]

In an age which celebrates individuality and fosters conflict, building sustainable communities is clearly a faith proposition. Yet developing a new way of living together will require even more than faith; it will require a radical willingness to abandon numerous habits, or what some would call "traditions". With this goal in mind, the search for the means by which a multi-cultural, multi-ethnic, multi-faith, and economically unequal global population can be persuaded to work together, even partially, has become the focus of those who struggle to build a viable form of sustainability.

[1]According to the *Dictionary of the Ecumenical Movement*, the term "sustainable society" was first used in the report of a working group of demographers, physical scientists, economists and theologians at the WCC world conference on science and technology for human development, in Bucharest, Romania, in 1974. Lossky, Nicholas, et al., eds., *Dictionary of the Ecumenical Movement* (Geneva: WCC Publications, 1991), p. 963.

[2]For a comprehensive recounting and analysis of the history of the WCC's use of the words "sustainable", "sustainability" and "development", see Larry Rasmussen's essay "Sustainable Development and Sustainable Community: Divergent Paths", in *Development Assessed: Ecumenical Reflections and Actions on Development*, Geneva: WCC Publications, 1995. Another extremely important source for understanding the development of the WCC's efforts to define sustainability can be found in the three reports issued by the Visser 't Hooft Foundation which emerged from three consultations at the Ecumenical Institute of Bossey on the themes of "Sustainable Growth (1993), "Work in Sustainable Societies" (1995), and "Sustainability and Globalisation" (1997); see *Sustainable Growth – A Contradiction in Terms? Economy, Ecology and Ethics After the Earth Summit* (Geneva: The Visser 't Hooft Endowment Fund for Leadership Development, 1993); Van Eldren, Martin, and Rob van Drimmelen, eds., "Work in a Sustainable Society", *Ecumenical Review* (48:269-391, July 1996); and de Santa Ana, Julio, ed., *Sustainability and Globalization* (Geneva: WCC Publications, 1998).

[3]*Ibid.*, p. 3.

[4]*Ibid.*, p. 1.

[5]WCC, *Now is the Time: The Final Document and Other Texts from the World Convocation on Justice, Peace and the Integrity of Creation, Seoul, Republic of Korea, 5-12 March 1990*, (Geneva: WCC Publications, 1990).

[6]*Ibid.*, p. 8.

[7]*Ibid.*, p. 18.

[8]*Ibid.*

[9]*Ibid.*

[10]*Ibid.*, p. 19.

[11]Rasmussen, Larry, "Sustainable Development and Sustainable Community: Divergent Paths" in *Development Assessed: Ecumenical Reflections and Actions on Development*; (Geneva: WCC Publications, 1995), p. 1.

[12]WCC, *Now is the Time: The Final Document and Other Texts from the World Convocation on Justice, Peace and the Integrity of Creation* (Geneva: WCC Publications, 1990), p. 9.

[13]WCC, *Searching for the New Heavens and the New Earth: An Ecumenical Response to UNCED* (Geneva: WCC Publications, 1992).

[14]*Ibid.*, p. 10.

[15]*Ibid.*, p. 13.

[16]*Ibid.*, p. 31.

[17]WCC, *Accelerated Climate Change: Sign of Peril, Test of Faith* (Geneva: WCC Publications, 1994).

[18]*Ibid.*, p. 13.

[19]*Ibid.*

[20]*Ibid.*, pp. 11-12.

[21]*Ibid.*, p. 13, Specific examples of this assertion can be found in the following statement: "God's concern for the whole of creation is revealed throughout scriptures. Instructions are given for the land itself to rest. In Leviticus 25:2, God gives people land, saying that the Earth itself must observe a Sabbath to the Lord. 'The fiftieth year shall be a Jubilee for you; do not sow and do not reap what grows of itself or harvest the untended vine' (Lev. 25:11). Failure to let the land rest and rejuvenate itself will lead to banishment (Lev. 26:35 and Chron. 36:21). The land was to be kept undefiled and unpolluted (Num. 35:33,34)".

[22]*Ibid.*, p. 25.

[23]*Ibid.*, pp. 13-14.

II

THE WCC AND THE CONSTRUCTION OF A NEW UNDERSTANDING OF SUSTAINABILITY AND DEVELOPMENT

Throughout its engagement with those who struggle to construct and implement viable forms of sustainable development, the World Council of Churches has remained consistent in its desire to elicit further debate and reflection on the meaning of the words "sustainable" and "development". Central to this desire is a recognition that the lines of debate have fallen into one of two camps: those who approach the sustainable development debate believing that the dictates of the market economy will always remain central to all models of sustainability and development, and those who believe that the requirements for the survival of the ecosphere, including all of its inhabitants, must determine the manner in which our economic, social, and political systems are governed. While the Council recognizes the preponderance of voices which ascribe to the first of these two models, its own cumulative statements clearly point to an allegiance with the second, or eco-centric model.

Given its position, the World Council must determine how it can most effectively engage those who place the priorities of the market above other considerations. In many cases, such actors are secular organizations or individuals who are disinclined to value the contribution of religious bodies, save for the most symbolic of exchanges. Recognizing the challenge these circumstances present, the WCC must consider the usefulness of having its own definition of "sustainable development" on hand when engaging such actors, despite its preference for the term "sustainable community". The usefulness bears itself out in the frequency with which "sustainable development" remains a defining term and the central focus of the majority of secular (as well as many religious) debates world wide. A WCC definition of "sustainable development" must therefore draw the clearest possible distinction between a market-driven understanding of sustainability and development and the Council's own vision. In order to respond to this task, it is first useful to draw together a summary of the Council's statements regarding "sustainability" and "development". This summation will then be followed by some recommendations of possible strategies that the Council might pursue in its efforts to influence the course of dialogues which place the term "sustainable development" at the centre of their deliberations.

ONE APPROACH TO DEFINING TERMS

The following is one possible synopsis of the Council's working definitions of "sustainable", "sustainability", and "development", which are either directly stated or implied in the WCC texts that have been cited thus far.

SUSTAINABLE/SUSTAINABILITY

"Sustainable" is clearly the most often used of the words under consideration. First associated with the term "sustainable society", the Council has often linked this word to quality of life considerations. These initially included population stability, renewable resources, economic continuity, technological innovation, and limits on material wealth.[1] In addition, the Council has also associated "sustainable" with human cooperation and community.[2] Later, the WCC came to use the word "sustainable" in reference to elements beyond human choice or control - in other words, the idea that the ecosphere itself is sustainable and could be a source of educating the Earth's human community as to the requirements of sustainability.[3]

What the Council describes as the requirements of "sustainability" are more often than not its preferred way of defining "sustainable". According to WCC statements, the requirements of sustainability include the following:

Sustainability requires a new definition of community. Sustainability requires humans to recognize that they are not the centre of creation as much as they are important members of a greater web of life.[4] To this end, sustainability requires human communities to understand their responsibility to and dependence upon the greater creation.[5] It requires new relationships between humans, between humans and non-humans, and between humans and their God.[6]

Sustainability requires human communities to recognize that an absence of justice will ensure an absence of sustainability.[7] Therefore, sustainability requires confession and repentance on the part of those who have colluded in the destruction of creation.[8] Sustainability is thus impossible in the absence of recognizing that the North has made far greater contributions to the destruction of the ecosphere than the South.[9] In order to accomplish these goals, sustainability will require heeding the wisdom of indigenous peoples.[10]

Sustainability requires the promotion of the spiritual and material well-being of Earth's inhabitants. Sustainability demands the spiritual and physical effort of a community which recognizes both its limitations and strengths.   Therefore, all such efforts must keep in mind that substantive progress toward sustainability will require faith and hope.[11]

DEVELOPMENT

The term "development" has occupied a place in the World Council's vocabulary even longer than "sustainable".[12] Like "sustainable", "development" was early on associated with the word "community" in WCC writings.[13] Later the Council's use of the term "development" came to be more often associated with a critique of the downside of economic expansion. More recently, the Council has once again become willing to employ "development" in non-pejorative ways, for example, in the context of "social development".

In many cases, the Council's definition of "development" is revealed in its descriptions of what development is not. In other cases, WCC documents positively suggest what development should entail. Via the documents thus far considered,[14] the World Council has made three central claims:

Development which deserves support builds community; therefore, development must promote a community ethic.[15] Proponents of development cannot make jobs, communities and the ecosystem secondary to maximizing profit.[16] For this reason, those undertaking development must recognize that humans exist within an ecosystem and that economics exists within human systems.[17]

Real development engenders justice. Development cannot be contingent on the marginalization of the human or non-human members of creation.[18] For this reason, development cannot reduce any member of creation to a monetary value.[19] At the same time, authentic development is not secured by pretending that all human communities possess the same opportunities to achieve their own economic security. Proponents of development must therefore clearly acknowledge the uneven playing field which now prevails, and thus recognize the distinction between the "luxury emissions of the rich and the survival emissions of the poor".[20]

True development always promotes the spiritual and material health of Earth's inhabitants. Development must therefore be understood as seeking to satisfy basic human needs, while at the same time addressing the material, social, and spiritual needs of creation's entire community.[21] To this end, development cannot engender a cult of money, a cult of performance, or a cult of instant gratification.[22] For this reason, authentic development does not discount values which cannot be expressed in economic terms.[23]

A SYNTHESIS OF TERMS

Having identified a number of definitions attributed to the words "sustainable", "sustainability", and "development" in a selection of WCC documents, our attention now turns to constructing a synthesis of these three terms. The aim of such an exercise is to offer one possible substantive definition for the combined term "sustainable development" which is in keeping with World Council statements. To this end, the following descriptions of "sustainable development" are drawn from combining the definitions and descriptions thus far offered. Each resulting definition (or "quality") of "sustainable development" contains elements from both a WCC definition of "sustainable" or "sustainability" along with a corresponding WCC definition of "development". [See Appendix I for the schematic on which this synthesis is built.] For example, the World Council has described "sustainability" as requiring "human communities to understand their responsibility to the greater creation".[24] In a similar vein, the documents examined described "development" as "recognizing that humans exist within an ecosystem".[25] Therefore, one possible description/definition of "sustainable development" could be the following: "sustainable development requires that human communities recognize that they exist within and are dependent upon a greater creation." While it is clearly impossible to offer in one sentence or phrase an adequate definition of "sustainable development", it is hoped that the reader can draw a cumulative definition from the following statements.

Truly sustainable development emphasizes an approach to economics which does not make jobs, communities or the ecosystem secondary to maximizing profit. It is at the same time an approach to economics which respects limits. Recognizing the importance of addressing the material needs of creation's entire community, sustainable development requires the human community to place an emphasis on the use of renewable resources. Therefore, sustainable development requires population stability, recognizing that humans exist within an ecosystem of limited resources. Because sustainable development does not engender a cult of money, it emphasizes the need for limits on material wealth. Respecting limits also entails yielding to precautionary actions to prevent environmental degradation. For this reason, truly sustainable development promotes technological innovation which seeks to satisfy basic human needs, while addressing the material needs of creation's entire community.

Truly sustainable development engenders a new definition of community. The social transformation which sustainable development requires must involve human communities recognizing that they are not the centre of creation, but are instead important members of a greater web of life. Sustainable development thus recognizes that the ecosphere is inherently self-sustaining, and is therefore a model for sustainable human communities. Sustainable development requires that human communities understand their responsibility to and dependence upon the greater creation within which they live. For this reason, truly sustainable development depends upon new relationships between humans, between humans and non-humans, and between humans and their God, which address the material, social and spiritual needs of creation's entire community. Sustainable development therefore requires a physical as well as spiritual effort, one which can only be found and sustained in community.

Truly sustainable development requires human communities to recognize that an absence of justice will ensure an absence of sustainability. For this reason, sustainable development will not marginalize the human or non-human members of creation. Because it does not marginalize any members of creation, truly sustainable development requires greater humanity to recognize the wisdom of indigenous peoples. Sustainable development is intrinsically tied to the promotion of just social transformation; it therefore requires confession and repentance by those who have colluded in creation's destruction, while distinguishing between the excesses of the North and the struggle for survival of the South.

Truly sustainable development promotes the spiritual and material well-being of all Earth's inhabitants. Such a project requires both spiritual effort and social transformation. Sustainable development therefore requires faith and hope, two things whose value cannot be expressed in monetary terms.

CHARTING A STRATEGY

While the above definitions are only a portion of the possible combinations of the terms "sustainable" and "development", they comprise one approach to arriving at a working WCC definition of sustainable development. And although agreement on what comprises the best of all possible definitions may rest in the future, it is important to consider in the short term what may be an even more critical question. The question is this: How does the World Council of Churches intend to maximize its influence in the greater global debate surrounding sustainable development? In addition, how can the positions the World Council has taken thus far on the subjects of sustainability and development be most effectively expressed outside the ecumenical community context?

The question of how to increase the Council's influence in shaping the sustainable development debate is justifiably a perennial concern of its members. While the Council's involvement on the international level (participating in UN-sponsored events and other international gatherings) remains a worthwhile pursuit, so too does the WCC's commitment to grass roots efforts. While strengthening the Council's presence on both of these fronts would no doubt increase visibility and underscore commitment, circumstances suggest that additional modifications of approach could also be useful.

Such modifications might focus on attempting to draw together the Council's numerous descriptions of its vision of sustainability and development into a more succinct package, based on a central anchoring claim. Among the possible central claims which can be drawn from the material thus far considered lies one particularly strong contender: "community". The hermeneutic of "community " or "sustainable community" is attractive for a number of reasons. It focuses on the preservation of something with which few would take issue. Secondly, "community", or more precisely "communities" affords the opportunity to broaden the conversation to include greater communities (i.e. non-human as well as human), as well as guard against the temptation by some to homogenize all people. For this reason, "communities" is an important term to include in any annotated definition of sustainable development. Most importantly, "communities" provides the descriptive linchpin for placing justice issues at the centre of the development debates.

Any talk of new frameworks, however, must first be anchored in the sober realization that the current dominant approach (which focuses on the centrality of the market economy as dictating the contours of sustainable development) is not waning in its influence. Given the dominant framework's continued popularity, the World Council is now being confronted with some of the limitations of its own approach thus far. If a new understanding of sustainable development is to have tangible impact in the greater international debates on sustainability, it will have to combine a strong and articulate critique of the injustices of the market economy with an aggressive, pro-active plan of action. Such a definition must therefore include concrete proposals for how society is to make the transition from current practices to a new manner of living and working together. In addition, given the unlikelihood of the market system disappearing in the near future, the Council's message must acknowledge its understanding of this fact or risk being dismissed by the majority of its potential audience.

A NEW UNDERSTANDING OF TERMS

The World Council's struggle to discern the most effective way of engaging those who insist on using the language of sustainable development will require careful consideration. In working toward this goal, a variety of central themes and supporting claims will have to be tested before any conclusion can be drawn. Although only a partial list of possibilities, the synthesis of the previously cited definitions and descriptions of sustainable development offers one way of approaching this task. Yet in order to ensure that the WCC's use of the term "sustainable development" most clearly reflects its own vision, the Council may be well advised to provide a definition which is leavened with its own emerging understanding of the term "sustainable communities". With this task in mind, the following is an attempt to use "sustainable communities" as an anchor, in order to provide a final synthesis which describes one possible value-based definition of sustainable development:

Truly sustainable development is not possible in the absence of sustainable communities, whose members recognize that they live within an ecosystem of limited resources. Sustainable development must therefore recognize that while global market systems currently make seeking economic gain necessary for survival, long-term survival cannot be secured if the importance of such gains is placed above communities, jobs, and the health of the ecosphere. Thus, truly sustainable development asks that we engender a willingness to enter into new relationships with humans, non-humans, and with God.

Truly sustainable development requires that human communities make the connection between justice and survival. Sustainable development is not possible if any group is held to be the centre, or relegated to the margins, of creation. Therefore, sustainable development requires the willingness to confess past transgressions and a belief in the possibility of social transformation.

Truly sustainable development recognizes that a spiritual life is not a luxury, but a prerequisite for the sustainability of all members of creation. While sustainable development cannot exist if individuals place their faith in money or self-satisfaction, sustainable development will thrive if communities model their economies on the needs, limits and lessons of the greater human and non-human creation. For this reason, truly sustainable development does not recognize values which can only be expressed in monetary terms.

Finally, sustainable development requires faith and hope. In a world which grows increasingly skeptical of the possibility of economic and social transformation, perhaps one of the most important elements the World Council of Churches can bring to the broader sustainable development debate is the gift of hope. Hope as a tangible asset is a topic that is rarely discussed among participants in international development gatherings. Yet as an entrée into descriptions of concrete plans of action, a voice of hope is an especially compelling contribution, and one which the World Council is uniquely qualified to provide.

In emphasizing the hermeneutic of sustainable communities while engaging those who debate the means of realizing a working definition of sustainable development, the WCC can provide a grounded, physical form to its vision of a more just future. By offering a clear definition of what it understands to be concrete and viable forms of sustainable communities, the WCC can articulately critique the underlying assumptions of the dominant economic models, while going beyond the role of the critic. This is because the vision of sustainable communities inherently implies the construction of something new and vital, which cannot be contained within the boundaries of an exclusively economic vocabulary. The work of defining and describing the concept of sustainable communities is therefore the task at hand and the focus of the following chapters.

[1]Lossky, Nicholas, et al., eds., *Dictionary of the Ecumenical Movement* (Geneva: WCC Publications, 1991), p. 963. These terms are all drawn from discussions which took place at the WCC World Conference on Science and Technology for Human Development, Bucharest, Romania, 1974.

[2]Rasmussen, Larry, "Sustainable Development and Sustainable Community: Divergent Paths", *Development Assessed: Ecumenical Reflections and Actions on Development* (Geneva: WCC Publications, 1995), p. 1.

[3]WCC, *Now is the Time: The Final Document and Other Texts from the World Convocation on Justice, Peace and the Integrity of Creation, Seoul, Republic of Korea*, 5-12 March 1990, (Geneva, WCC Publications, 1990), p. 18.

[4]WCC, *Searching for the New Heavens and the New Earth:: An Ecumenical Response to UNCED* (Geneva: WCC Publications, 1992), p. 13.

[5]WCC, *Now is the Time*, p. 8.

[6]WCC, *Searching for the New Heavens*, p. 31.

[7]WCC, *Now is the Time*, p. 19.

[8]WCC, *Accelerated Climate Change: Sign of Peril, Test of Faith* (Geneva: WCC Publications, 1994), p. 14.

[9]*Ibid.*, pp. 11-12.

[10]WCC, *A Report of the Delegation of the World Council of Churches and the Lutheran World Federation to the Third Session of the UN Commission on Sustainable Development* (Geneva: WCC Publications, 1995), p.11.

[11]WCC, *Now is the Time*, p. 9.

[12]Rasmussen, "Sustainable Development and Sustainable Community: Divergent Paths", p. 3.

[13]*Ibid.*, p. 3.

[14]Some of the following information is also drawn from *A Report of the Delegation of the WCC and the Lutheran World Federation to the Third Session of the UN Commission on Sustainable Development*.

[15]*Ibid.*, p. 25, from a reflection by Gunnar Heiene.

[16]*Ibid.*, p. 20, from a reflection by James Sullivan.

[17]*Ibid.*

[18]WCC, *Accelerated Climate Change*, p. 13.

[19]From a reflection by James Sullivan in *A Report of the Delegation*.

[20]WCC, *Accelerated Climate Change*, pp. 11-12.

[21]From a reflection by Gunnar Heiene in *A Report of the Delegation*, p. 17.

[22]*Ibid.*, p. 25.

[23]From a reflection by James Sullivan in *A Report of the Delegation*, p. 20.

[24]WCC, *Now is the Time*, p. 8.

[25]WCC, *A Report of the Delegation*, p. 20.

III
DEFINING SUSTAINABLE COMMUNITIES – A BASIS FOR CONVERSATION: LARRY RASMUSSEN'S *EARTH COMMUNITY, EARTH ETHICS* AND JAMES CONE'S "WHOSE EARTH IS IT ANYWAY?" AS A FOUNDATION FOR ANALYSIS

Just as we saw in the conversations surrounding "sustainable development", efforts to define "sustainable communities" likewise remain an unfinished work. While no one voice or group of voices can be exclusively privileged to construct an understanding of "sustainable communities", insightful efforts have been made which provide a useful foundation. Two important examples are Larry Rasmussen's *Earth Community, Earth Ethics* and James Cone's "Whose Earth is it Anyway?"

Earth Community, Earth Ethics charts the interplay between the physical, social, economic, political and theological dimensions of "earth's distress".[1] At the same time, Rasmussen engages in the constructive task of naming beliefs and behaviours that build sustainable communities. In order to provide a basis for further analysis, let us consider Rasmussen's primary points around two questions: (1) What promotes sustainable communities? and (2) What undermines sustainable communities?

For clarity's sake, Rasmussen's observations will be divided into four areas: physical sustainability, social sustainability, political/economic sustainability, and theological sustainability. While these four overlap, the distinctions will be useful in focusing subsequent analysis.

WHAT PROMOTES SUSTAINABLE COMMUNITIES?

THE PHYSICAL DIMENSION

According to Rasmussen, the following beliefs and actions help us to understand and promote the physical dimension of sustainable communities:

The well-being of Earth is primary; human well-being is derivative.[2] Earth, including humankind, is one contiguous community, a fact which is perhaps the most significant scientific discovery of the twentieth century – i.e. all that exists, coexists.[3] For this reason, humans must recognize that the Earth is the bone of our bone and the flesh of our flesh.[4]

"Ecological" knowing means understanding the interrelated dynamics that make up the total life of *Oikumene* (the whole inhabited world) and the requirements for living together.[5] Diversity breeds stability, adaptability and, through these qualities, fosters sustainability.[6] Sustainablity's moral framework should therefore build upon Aldo Leopold's categorical imperative: "A thing is right when it tends to preserve the integrity, stability, and beauty of the biotic community, and it is wrong when it tends otherwise".[7]

Earth's treasures are not an unlimited resource but a one-time endowment, essentially a closed system that must sustain itself or die.[8] All human activity is therefore conducted within the context of an "economics of borrowing", with repercussions beyond any immediate context.[9] Nature is not simply a "big bank of resources" standing at the ready; it is the source and teacher of the very designs we must draw upon in order to address the problems we face. Yet recognizing that Earth is a closed system is not enough. We must also keep in mind that all of Earth's creatures live within a system which constantly fluctuates and evolves in ways that defy easy measurement. For this reason, determining the true dimensions of Earth's carrying capacity is impossible. The human community would therefore be wise to err on the side of low (rather than high) estimates of what Earth's community can withstand in the way of human impact .[10]

THE SOCIAL DIMENSION

According to Rasmussen, the beliefs and actions which help us to understand and promote the social dimension of sustainable communities include the following:

Sustainability owes as much to its socio-ethical character as it does to its technical prowess and knowledge base.[11] Sustainability will therefore not be achieved through exclusively material means. It will be realized only when the social and cultural health of communities is given the same level of attention now lavished on their technological and economic development. Our current lack of sustainability is in many respects a crisis of culture – a culture that is unsustainable, in part due to our collective unwillingness to submit human power to grace and humility.[12]

Sustainability is built from the ground up, first within individual communities and then across communities.[13] In turn, sustainability is dynamic; different communities have different needs and wishes for their social, economic, and political future.[14] Sustainability must therefore be pursued with these facts in mind, and should be guided by an ethic of community which recognizes the unique circumstances of individual communities, while maintaining the entire biotic community as its scope.[15]

Social and environmental justice are integrally related.[16] "Justice" is not a synonym for simple numerical equality; it is a collective *mutuality* in which we share one another's fate and promote one another's well-being.[17] The starting point of sustainable community is therefore found in the act of entering into the predicaments of those who suffer, for compassion (suffering with) is the passion of life itself.[18] Justice is served when our communities live out such tangible compassion, while embracing the implicit moral norms of sustainability: participation, sufficiency, equity, accountability, material simplicity, spiritual richness, responsibility and subsidiarity.[19]

THE POLITICAL AND ECONOMIC DIMENSION

According to Rasmussen, the beliefs and actions which help us to understand and promote the political and economic dimension of sustainable community include the following:

The Northern concept of "progress" has failed.[20] Many of those thought to be "realists" (including many businesspeople, economists, politicians and diplomats) have exposed themselves as naïve utopians, through their insistence that current economic and political practices will ultimately produce environmental sustainability, a more equitable distribution of goods and services, and a higher level of prosperity for the majority of the Earth's inhabitants.[21] The human economy must come closer to reflecting the fact that the market is only a subset of the economy of earth.[22] Therefore, economic policies should reflect the fact that greater creation depends on diversity, thrives on difference, and perishes in the imbalance of uniformity.[23] For this reason, "modern" agricultural practices are an impediment to sustainability: we must remember that no one can live in a "post-agricultural world."[24]

Long-term sustainability is diminished by export-oriented short-term profit. Sustainability is affirmed by local production from local resources for local use by those who have made a life investment in the immediate locale.[25] Those who call for a return to focussing on local production for local consumption are often accused of looking backward rather than facing the realities of globalization. Yet those who claim that long-term sustainability can be secured by simply relying on heightened trade, emerging energy technologies and individual lifestyle changes may be the most naïve of all. Authentic sustainability will require more profound commitments to change than many analysts are willing to concede. This is because long-term sustainability will demand a reconceptualization and transformation of the economic system itself, guided by a new vision and definition of community.[26] Truly long-term sustainability will never be realized by purely market-driven forces.

Justice and equality are central to establishing and maintaining sustainability.[27] The concentration of wealth among a small number of people is responsible for 70% of global environmental degradation. Such a concentration of wealth has not only contributed to the growing gap between the rich and the poor, it has also contributed to the polarization and fragmentation of communities across the North-South split. Any power that does not go to the places where community and creation are most obviously ruptured and ruined has no power for healing at all.[28] Enterprises which constructively contribute to genuine community must therefore regard all people not simply as individuals, but as persons-in-community who require a living wage, real health care, a clean environment, and consumer protections.[29] At the same time, building sustainable communities requires that each community soberly assess the carrying capacity of its own geographic locale and strive to live within its limits. Sustainability cannot be imported from another location in the form of goods and services, in order to make up for the ecological inefficiency of one's own community.[30] Such practices are all too often the source of others' impoverishment.

Sustainability requires providing a space and time for people to begin to envision the future they desire for their own communities, and ensuring that these same communities have access to the power to build from their vision.[31] This goal can only be realized when the needs of the household, which seeks to maximize the quality of life and benefits of its members, are given priority over the needs of the corporation, which measures success in terms of maximized profits and market share.[32] Our decision-making mechanisms should therefore be more closely informed by the notion of subsidiarity, which holds that whatever does not imperatively need to be decided at higher levels should be decided at the most local level possible.[33] While respecting the rights of the individual, local communities should not, however, be limited to the human realm. The locations and purposes of the Earth's non-human species should likewise not be manipulated or altered to accommodate economic or political goals. Such manipulation runs counter to the fact that each species within Earth's community occupies a particular "niche" role, which is foundational to long-term sustainability.[34]

THE THEOLOGICAL DIMENSION

Rasmussen observes that the beliefs and actions which help us to understand and promote the theological dimension of sustainable communities include the following:

God has repeatedly called upon ordinary and ostensibly powerless people to subvert deeply entrenched powers and help effect a new world.[35] From the Hebrew people breaking free from Pharaoh's slavery to the ranks of the marginalized who were transformed as they followed Jesus, the God of the Hebrew Bible and the Christian Testament is clearly one who subverts all assumptions regarding power. These divine acts of redefining power are works of extraordinary creativity, which repeatedly inspired human communities to suspend their disbelief and live as they had never done before. Such is the basis of the faith that will be required for the building of authentic sustainability.

Turning to God is simultaneously a turning to Earth.[36] Sustainability is cultivated through a sense of awe and reverence before the goodness and grandeur of the whole created order.[37] The love of God is often tactile. It is for this reason that experiencing the grace of God requires falling in love with Earth and sticking around.[38] This is because redemption does not occur in the context of an Earth-denying asceticism, but through an immersion in the very sphere reclaimed by God's redemptive work, for there is no Heaven without Earth.[39]

Sustainable communities are embodied through a faith that resists the actual in the name of the possible, while fighting the three great instabilities: injustice, "unpeace" and creation's disintegration.[40] Jesus' crucifixion should have been the last one, but it was not. To follow Jesus means vigorously resisting the powers of oppression and degradation.[41] We must therefore come to define faith as the capacity to affirm life in the midst and face of death, to be reconciled to its limits (including the tragic limits of the human condition), and to accept the whole without despair.[42]

Religion *can* **effect our conversion to sustainable communities, but not without significant reform.**[43] Such reform must come to include defining religion's task as being that of loudly and publicly denying that justice is a mirage.[44] At the same time, we must remember that any religion that loses touch with the natural world will grow indifferent toward it and be susceptible to sanctioning the abuse of it.[45] For this reason, the three following acts should be understood as sin:(1) the refusal to act as responsible representatives of God (*imago dei*) who value the lives and well-being of other members of creation, (2) the injustice of grabbing more than is one's due, and (3) the arrogance of treating the Earth and its inhabitants as property at one's disposal.[46]

In the struggle to change long held habits and traditions, humans must look for new sources of guidance and wisdom. Looking to the designs found in greater creation is one critical avenue to explore in pursuing this task. Yet while nature is always a teacher, it is not always a teacher of morality. For this reason, human beings, as a part of nature, cannot escape their distinctive work as moral creatures, for morality is as crucial to sustainability as the ability to understand nature's basic designs.[47]

WHAT UNDERMINES SUSTAINABLE COMMUNITIES?

THE PHYSICAL AND SOCIAL DIMENSION

According to Rasmussen, the physical and social dimension of what undermines sustainable communities includes these behaviours and beliefs:

Sustainable communities are undermined through the belief that humans are the logical source of all meaningful standards and measurements. Sustainability is undermined when we believe that social well-being can always be measured by a rising or falling GDP and, by implication, that commerce is the most tangible path to human liberation.[48] An equally problematic standard of measurement is grounded in the assumption that time itself is a strictly human invention, which can be divorced from greater creation and its requirements for regeneration, which have their own time lines.[49]

Sustainable communities are undermined whenever we choose to divide humankind from otherkind and humans from one another – this is apartheid thinking.[50] Such divisions go hand in hand with a willingness to reduce all non-human and many human members of creation to the role of "resources" or "natural capital."[51] In the final analysis, sustainable communities are most often undermined by those who believe that an unjust society is worth sustaining.[52]

THE ECONOMIC AND POLITICAL DIMENSION

Rasmussen observes that the economic and political dimension of what undermines sustainable communities is expressed through the following interrelated set of beliefs and actions, which include:

Sustainability is undermined through the belief that perpetual growth and technological advancement are always natural, good, inevitable and ecologically viable.[53] Sustainability is undermined by embracing the "frontier paradigm" which holds that there is plenty of the desired good "over the next hill".[54] In the same vein, the belief that Earth's distress can be resolved through the discovery of superior technology, rather than through the recognition that Earth's distress is a crisis of culture, only lends to the illusions which undermine sustainability.[55]

Sustainability is undermined through the belief that an increasingly globalized economy will necessarily result in a more equitable distribution of power, goods and services,[56] **and that economic development should be the organizing principle of all societies and nations.**[57] The fact that a sizable percentage of the world's jobs are dependent upon a globalized economy is descriptive of a phenomenon which has often lead to unsustainability.[58] Sustainability is further undermined by the belief that the quarterly earnings report is *the* bottom line.[59] Such a belief only serves to affirm the practice of privatizing profits while socializing costs.[60]

Sustainable communities are undermined through the unequal distribution of economic and political power, which is nearly always sustained by the exploitation and depletion of human and non-human resources.[61] The political colonization of the two-thirds world by a handful of Northern nation-states has been replaced by an economic hegemony which is far more effective in its ability to control and manipulate than previously known arrangements.[62] The ascendance of the corporation (and particularly the multi-national corporation) over against the relative power of governments to impact economic, political and social policy formation at the national, regional and even local level has changed the political landscape.[63] Such trends have only served to promote the belief that it is acceptable to appropriate other peoples' sustainability to meet one's own perceived resource needs.[64] This belief is clearly reflected in the continued willingness of political and economic leaders to engage in environmental racism, forcing non-white and/or poor people to bear the brunt of Earth's distress.[65]

THE THEOLOGICAL DIMENSION

Finally, Rasmussen describes the theological dimension of what undermines sustainable communities as residing in the following belief systems and practices:

Holding on to anthropocentric theologies prevents humans from seeing their intrinsic relation to non-human creation and its inherent integrity.[66] This problem is only furthered by the inability of the political and economic leadership of many nation-states (principally those among the industrialized nations) to recognize the world as a holy mystery and a gift, and to stand in awe of greater creation.[67]

These elements of sustainable and unsustainable communities provide a basis for further analysis. It is nonetheless necessary to turn to another foundational document, in order to more fully explore what Rasmussen has identified as one of the greatest enemies of sustainable communities: the practice of environmental racism.

"WHOSE EARTH IS IT ANYWAY?"[68]

James Cone is clear in naming one of the most pernicious sources of global imbalance: the continued vitality of white supremacy.

> Do we have any reason to believe that the culture most responsible for the ecological crisis will also provide the moral and intellectual resources for the earth's liberation?..... I have a deep suspicion about the theological and ethical values of the white culture and religion. For five hundred years whites have acted as if they owned the world's resources and have forced people of color to accept their scientific and ethical values.[69]

Cone's observations are an invitation to consider anew how even the most sincere and non-coercive Northern efforts vis-à-vis the global and/or economic South might be received. At the same time, Cone challenges those who begin and end their analysis of ecological degradation in terms of the pursuit of capital, by claiming that the so-called bottom line is not simply about money, but a different type of logic which is not always openly named by its proponents and beneficiaries:

> It is a mechanistic and instrumental logic that defines everything and everybody in terms of their contribution to the development and defense of white world supremacy.[70]

Cone asks hard questions which white people, *and those who claim for themselves similarly disproportionate privileges*, need to answer.

> Many ecologists speak often of the need for humility and mutual dialogue. They tell us that we are all interrelated and interdependent, including human and otherkind. ...If white ecologists really believe that, why do most still live in segregated communities? ...Why is there so much talk of love, humility, interrelatedness, and interdependence, and yet so little of these values reflected in white people's dealings with people of color?[71]

Such contradictions merit consideration, especially among Northerners whose work entails persuading those from groups other than their own to adopt different life practices vis-à-vis greater creation. At the same time, Cone's observations serve to name beliefs and behaviours which either promote or undermine sustainable communities.

WHAT PROMOTES SUSTAINABLE COMMUNITIES?

According to Cone, the following beliefs and practices serve to promote sustainable communities:

We must recognize and act on the fact that racism and poverty are ecological issues.[72] Economic and political practices which place the poor and/or people of colour in the most polluted and physically dangerous workplaces can never be tolerated.[73] Authentic sustainability therefore demands that we live our lives as people who understand that saving the lives of people of colour in the ghettos and prisons is at least as important as saving the habitats of particular non-human species.[74] Such practices go hand in hand with acknowledging the simple fact that if something is not safe enough to be dumped in one's own neighbourhood or country, it is not safe enough to be dumped in someone else's neighbourhood or country.[75]

Sustainable communities cannot be built in the absence of a sustained critique and a struggle to amend the culture most responsible for the environmental crisis.[76] As Audre Lorde wrote, "The master's tools will never dismantle the master's house", for such tools are too narrow and thus assume that people of colour have nothing to say about race, gender, sexuality, and the Earth – all of which are interconnected.[77] It is therefore essential to consider again Martin Luther King Jr.'s image of the Beloved Community as a powerful symbol for those who struggle to build community across boundaries of difference, for as King wrote: "All life is interrelated, whatever affects one directly affects all indirectly (because) there is an interrelated structure of reality."[78] Thus, only when white people and others of extraordinary privilege realize that a fight against racism and poverty is a fight for *their own* humanity will it be possible to create a coalition of people of all colours in the struggle to save the biosphere.[79]

While white supremacy is clearly Cone's principle explanation of what serves to most readily undermine sustainable communities, his observations serve to hold up some additional critical questions. Perhaps one of the most important of these is found in the following observation:

> For over five hundred years, through the wedding of science and technology, white people have been exploiting nature and killing people of color in every nook and cranny of the planet in the name of God and democracy.[80]

Who is the God we serve? What does (S)He look like? Does the appearance of the God we image in our minds help or hinder our efforts at building sustainability across boundaries of difference? It would seem that by the obvious fact that Jesus was not a European, white people would have long ago found it morally difficult to claim so much as their own. Worshipping someone who does not share one's own racial identification would logically make it hard to exploit people who look different in Jesus' name, or so it would seem. The implications which follow the fact that Jesus was not white, however, represent a set of ideas that only a small percentage of white people are willing to fully consider, and quite reluctantly at that.

James Cone challenges white people to acknowledge how white the majority of global decision makers really are. For example, how often do Northerners acknowledge the colour of the majority of those who guide the World Bank, the International Monetary Fund, the World Trade Organization, the G-7 nations, those who hold the overwhelming majority of permanent seats on the Security Council of the United Nations, or the majority of CEOs and stockholders of the world's most powerful multi-national corporations? Whether or not many Northerners have noticed the near-uniformity of the racial makeup of these leaders, one can be sure that it has not been lost on many other people. While change in the direction of more inclusivity seems daunting to many, it is clear that nothing will change until people of privilege, particularly those who are white, become willing to talk about such things openly and honestly, and then turn to giving up a significant portion of their power.

While Cone's pronouncements clearly lend themselves to broad scale conversations, his message also invites personal reflection. Some of the questions suggested by his remarks include the following: Who is *really* our neighbour? With whom do we share our meals (and not simply a ritualized meal in a church, but those that take place in our homes)? Do our claims of interconnectedness truly extend to those of different races, or merely to non-human creation? Are we willing to change as much as we are willing to ask others to change? Are we willing to fight for the rights of those of different races, genders, ethnicities, classes, castes and religions as passionately as we are willing to fight for other members of God's Creation? And finally, how much power are those of us in a position of privilege willing to let go of?

Larry Rasmussen and James Cone have offered a set of observations, recommendations and questions that merit careful consideration. They can be used as a basis to analyze other texts that further define sustainable communities. In examining the following WCC documents, we must identify how the work of others can expand the vision which Rasmussen and Cone have offered.

[1]Rasmussen, Larry, *Earth Community, Earth Ethics* (Maryknoll, NY: Orbis Books, 1996), p. 7. Rasmussen borrows this phrase from a 1928 address by Dietrich Bonhoeffer: "Earth and its distress – that is the Christian's Song of Songs." See, Bonhoeffer, Dietrich, "Grundfragen einer christlichen Ethik." *Gesammelte Schriften* (Munich: Kaiser, 1966), 3:57-58; trans. L. Rasmussen.
[2]*Ibid.*, p. 30.
[3]*Ibid.*, p. 15..
[4]*Ibid.*, p. xii.
[5]*Ibid.*, p. 93..
[6]*Ibid.*, p. 114.
[7]*Ibid.*, p. 345 see Aldo Leopold, *A Sand County Almanac* (New York: Ballantine, 1970), p. 262.
[8]*Ibid.*, p. 102.
[9]*Ibid.*, p. 103.
[10]*Ibid.*, p. 157.
[11]*Ibid.*, p. 42.
[12]*Ibid.*, pp. 7-8.
[13]*Ibid.*, p. 343.
[14]*bid.*, p. 145.
[15]*Ibid.*, p. 108.
[16]*Ibid.*, p. 103.
[17]*Ibid.*, p. 260.
[18]*Ibid.*, pp. 261, 284-285.
[19]*Ibid.*, pp. 172-173.
[20]*Ibid.*, p. 180
[21]*Ibid.*, pp. 152-153.
[22]*Ibid.*, pp. 111-112.
[23]*Ibid.*, p. 114.
[24]*Ibid.*, p. p. 57.
[25]*Ibid.*, p. 123.
[26]*Ibid.*, p. 144.
[27]*Ibid*, p. 42.
[28]*Ibid.*, pp. 286-287.
[29]*Ibid.*, p. 145.
[30]*Ibid.*, p. 339.
[31]*Ibid.*, p. 338. See Stephen Viederman, "The Economics of Sustainability: Challenges" 17 (This paper is available from the Jessie Smith Noyes Foundation, New York, New York).
[32]*Ibid.*, *Earth Community, Earth Ethics*, p. 92.
[33]*Ibid.*, pp. 172-173.
[34]*Ibid.*, p. 114.
[35]*Ibid.*, p. 252.
[36]*Ibid.*, p. 110.
[37]*Ibid*, p. 145.
[38]*Ibid.*, pp. 280-281.
[39]*Ibid.*, pp. 256, 207.
[40]*Ibid.*, p. 227.
[41]*Ibid*, pp. 292-293.
[42]*Ibid.*, p. 277.
[43]*Ibid.*, p. 10.
[44]*Ibid.*, p. 184.
[45]*Ibid.*, p. 193.

[46]*Ibid.*, p. 293.
[47]*Ibid.*, p. 347.
[48]*Ibid.*, pp. 149, 225.
[49]*Ibid.*, p. 34.
[50]*Ibid.*, pp. xii, 32.
[51]*Ibid.*, p. 33.
[52]*Ibid.*, p. 139
[53]*Ibid.*, p. 51.
[54]*Ibid.*, p. 123.
[55]*Ibid.*, pp. 7-8.
[56]*Ibid.*, p. 15.
[57]*Ibid.*, p. 43.
[58]*Ibid.*, p. 117.
[59]*Ibid.*, p. 15.
[60]*Ibid.*, p. 118.
[61]*Ibid.*, p. 42.
[62]*Ibid.*, p. 62.
[63]*Ibid.*, p. 63.
[64]*Ibid.*, p. 104.
[65]*Ibid.*, p. 77.
[66]*Ibid.*, pp. 35-36.
[67]*Ibid.*, pp. 62-63.
[68]Cone, James H., "Whose Earth is It Anyway?", *Risks of Faith:: The Emergence of a Black Theology of Liberation, 1968-1998* (Boston: Beacon Press, 1999).
[69]*Ibid.*, p. 143.
[70]*Ibid.*, p. 138.
[71]*Ibid.*, p. 144.
[72]*Ibid.*, p. 141.
[73]*Ibid.*
[74]*Ibid.*, p. 145.
[75]This comment is drawn from the observations of Bishop Frederick C. James, as cited by James Cone, *ibid.*, p. 141.
[76]*Ibid.*, p. 142.
[77]*Ibid.*, p. 144. For the full text which Cone cites, see Lorde, Audre, *Sister Outsider* (Tumansburg, NY: Crossing Press, 1984), p. 110.
[78]This passage is drawn from an earlier version of Cone's essay, see Cone, James H., "Whose Earth is It Anyway?" Hessel, Dieter, and Larry Rasmussen, eds., *Earth Habitat: Eco-Justice and the Church's Response* (Minneapolis: Fortress Press, 2001).
[79]Cone, "Whose Earth is It Anyway?", *Risks of Faith*, p. 145.
[80]Cone, "Whose Earth is It Anyway?" *Earth Habitat*.

IV.
BUILDING SUSTAINABLE COMMUNITIES WITHIN THE CONTEXT OF A GLOBALIZED ECONOMY: A SELECTION OF STATEMENTS BY THE WORLD COUNCIL OF CHURCHES AND ITS FRIENDS, 1997-1998

Rasmussen and Cone make it quite clear that any practical definition of sustainable communities will not be realized in a vacuum. Rather, building sustainable community must take place in many different contexts and in the face of extraordinary and varied opposition. The following is a compendium of some of the primary documents the World Council has recently published, which attempt to describe some of the realities which any builder of sustainable community is forced to encounter. While these documents are clearly part of a greater work in progress, they offer a number of critical descriptions which interpret current circumstances and prescribe strategies of response. This chapter will identify selected themes from these documents and divide them into three categories: (1) the values and assumptions of sustainability and its counterpart, the dominant development model, (2) sustainable communities within the economics of globalization, and (3) building the communities in which we honestly intend to live.

THE VALUES AND ASSUMPTIONS OF SUSTAINABILITY AND ITS COUNTERPART, THE DOMINANT DEVELOPMENT MODEL

The WCC's ongoing commitment to the issue of climate change has produced a number of documents, including the 1998 *Climate Change and the Quest for Sustainable Societies.*[1] The authors of Climate Change make it clear that any efforts toward building sustainability must include a sober assessment of the values and assumptions of the dominant development model, which are expressed in its definitions of the terms "progress", "work" and "rest":

> The idea of progress is...the cause of a distorted understanding of growth. In living nature, growth is a matter of either healthy or bad – cancer like – development, and is always accompanied by the expectation of fertility in the phase of saturation. In Western culture, however, economic growth simply means (in principle) the unlimited expansion of production and acquisition.....
>
> These distortions point to an even deeper pattern of Western culture – the distorted balance between work and rest. Rest means taking distance from work achieved. Taking distance is essential for the fulfillment of life. Without distance the importance of work tends to be overestimated (and) haste rules life.[2]

According to *Climate Change*, a second source of opposition to sustainability is found in the dominant development model's emphasis on "measurability", which assigns value to a very narrow range of people, behaviours and non-human creatures:

> What is not measurable is generally regarded as unreal. Efficiency, for instance, tends to be defined as the surplus money value obtained by measurable output in comparison with measurable input and costs. In such a culture, the simple fact that not everything is measurable tends to be overlooked. What upholds and sustains life but cannot be measured is often treated as irrelevant.[3]

Climate Change argues that the logic of measurability is fortified by a third source of opposition to sustainability, which its authors call the "primacy of use over against respect for otherness".[4] The "primacy of use" world view values non-human creation as almost exclusively an economic resource. And, echoing the observations of James Cone, the "primacy of use" interpretation of human creation reduces human beings from non-dominant cultures to an economic value.

> People of other cultures are primarily seen as potential participants in the worldwide system. They are valued by their economic potential. In the name of global economy, the value of existing life patterns which have been meaningful for many generations is of subordinate significance.[5]

Finally, *Climate Change* points out that any credible efforts toward building sustainability will have to be made in opposition to the Northern "mechanistic world view". Such a view holds that markets, and even democracies, are mechanisms with "an in-built feedback capacity, ...capable of restoring equilibrium as soon as they are threatened by outside forces".[6] In this view, the solution to most problems is found in increased economic or political competition. For this reason, the mechanistic view defines "faith" as a belief in the abiding health, well-being and wisdom of the market itself.

Over against the values and assumptions of the dominant economic model, how should the builders of sustainable communities describe sustainability's values and assumptions? According to *Climate Change*, such values and assumptions are expressed in the following statements:

Development of the Life of the People: No realistic economic development is imaginable which is not intrinsically related to the life of people, to their needs, to their styles of living and to their range of responsibilities.[7] Thus, the fundamental criterion for the development of technology and economy has to be the responsible human community.[8] Regional and local diversity needs to be recognized economically as well as culturally.[9] Human values like care, social responsibility and respect for public interest will more easily develop within communities than in processes guided by the sole principle of economic growth.[10] None of these goals will be possible in the absence of recognizing the wisdom of Southern and Indigenous cultures, which must become an intrinsic part of domestic and international economic decision making.[11]

Maturity Expressed through the Recognition of Limits: No healthy development of economic life is possible without the recognition of limits. The present orientation towards maximum increases of standards of living betrays an element of immaturity. Maturity presupposes some degree of control over desires, especially if these desires are harmful to others.[12]

Redefining "Sound Investment": More investments must be made in human and social capital, which are life-sustaining expenditures, thus preventing harm to human and non-human creation and improving both health conditions and educational opportunities.[13] Such investment practices must be centred on naming the real cost of all monetary and material transactions. Pricing must therefore reflect the real costs involved in present economic activities, in terms of both human and non-human impact.[14]

Finally, *Climate Change* offers a fruit tree as a metaphor for explaining a sustainable way of understanding growth, and makes these observations: First, the growth of a tree involves all cells, just as building sustainability requires that all members of a community participate. Secondly, the growth of a tree is dependent upon its relationship to the soil as it adapts to available conditions, just as human communities will collapse if they do not care about the ground on which they are built. Finally, every tree knows that it will not be possible to blossom and bear fruit without restricting its expansion, and thus a tree does not seek to grow into heaven. Humans could learn from this lesson by defining fertility in terms of fulfilling people's basic needs, rather than the maximization of production and exports.[15]

Effectively countering the values and assumptions of the dominant development model requires clear thinking and even clearer explanations by the advocates of sustainability. The authors of *Climate Change* provide a sound foundation for building a vocabulary of engagement, which can serve to directly and publicly question what many refer to as the idolatrous theology of the dominant economic model.[16] Now that some of the themes of such a dialogue have been identified, let us now turn to a series of WCC documents which place the building of sustainable communities within the current context.

FOUR PERSPECTIVES ON SUSTAINABLE COMMUNITY WITHIN THE ECONOMICS OF GLOBALIZATION: DICKINSON, DE SANTA ANA, BATISTA AND ADDY

Richard Dickinson

The international impact of the dominant Northern model of development is often described by the term "globalization". While the concept of globalization is associated with multiple events, movements and conflicts, Richard Dickinson, in his 1998 document *Economic Globalization: Deepening Challenge for Christians*,[17] identifies six basic factors which provide a sound basis for describing globalization's form:

Burgeoning New Technologies: The increased sophistication of communications technologies, including computers and the rising importance of the Internet, have helped dominant economic actors to extend their influence and rapidly shift currencies from one market to another.[18]

Mergers and Longitudinal Integration: Transnational corporations, particularly in the North, are merging and concentrating power at an unprecedented rate, diminishing competition in economically weaker nation-states, and in some cases (such as Sub-Saharan Africa) excluding entire regions altogether.[19]

New Global Institutions Controlled by Free-Market Agents: The World Trade Organization, the International Monetary Fund, and the attempt to ratify and implement the Multilateral Agreement on Investment are all examples of some of the most powerful Northern actors working to maintain their dominance in international economic competition.[20]

The Diminishment of the Power of the Nation-State: Today, corporations are far less bound by the geographic borders of a particular nation or region, and are instead more defined by the rules, practices and guiding values of the international market place. Consequently, sovereign states have less and less control over the economic realities within their borders.[21]

Growing Economic Disparities: While it was argued that the freeing of market forces would benefit the poorest segments of the global population, empirical evidence contradicts this claim. United Nations Development Programme statistics for 1992 concluded that 20% of the world's inhabitants who live in wealthy countries receive 82% of the world's income, while the bottom 20% receive 1.4% of the world's income. The wealthy average 60 times the income of the poor, and the gap has doubled since 1950.[22]

The Increasing Debt of Poorer Countries: The IMF's Structural Adjustment Programmes, based on free-market assumptions which often had little to do with the specific circumstances of borrower states, have diminished many nations' capacities to participate in their own economic renewal.[23]

In the introduction to Dickinson's text, Sam Kobia identifies three challenges for the ecumenical movement in facing the realities of globalization: (1) to identify an alternative explanation of the global reality, (2) to define and build sustainability in the face of neo-liberal models of development, and (3) to articulate an alternative vision of the unity of humankind.[24] These challenges are clearly shared by any who work to build sustainable communities. Yet before any building takes place, it is useful to first consider the state of communities within the current context of globalization.

Julio de Santa Ana

In his book *Sustainability and Globalization*, Julio de Santa Ana points out some of the contradictions between the guiding values of many communities and the type of community globalization favours:

> The social relationships which globalization favours are those which are "virtual" and less personal. That is, that prevailing trends of the global economy privilege that which is more characteristic of the life of mass society – mass communications, — mass consumption, homogenization of patterns of life, mass culture.[25]

De Santa Ana describes the "homogenization of human behavior" globalization encourages as a phenomenon which "endangers community life by threatening people's relationships with their own cultures and by depersonalizing human relationships."[26] At the same time, de Santa Ana points out, globalization offers a new theology and a new definition of the role of humanity which may pose its greatest threat to the health and longevity of existing communities:

> The complacency of the comfortable can easily become a form of idolatry. Without thinking about it, they passively allow the market to assume the properties and dimensions of God in their imaginations and in their behaviour. People come to accept the fate meted out by the market as if submission were the only option. Thus what is in actuality a mere mechanism devised by human beings to foster efficient production and consumption takes on the proportions of an autonomous force governing the lives of individuals and communities.[27]

In this observation, Julio de Santa Ana has offered a clear description of one of the primary spiritual challenges of globalization. By identifying a primary source of the "theology of unsustainability", de Santa Ana helps to prepare sustainable communities' advocates for the reality of what they are fighting to change.

Building sustainable communities is not an exclusively theological undertaking. With this in mind, de Santa Ana cautions that people of faith should concede that their own efforts at building sustainability must take place in a world of competing forces, which require negotiation and compromise:

> Just as Christians must not succumb to the temptation of idolatry, so they should not be misled by romantic and idealistic visions of a perfect state of things. There is no perfect society.

> Though obliged to unmask and resist the idolatry inherent in the present system, Christians should not suppose or suggest that there will ever be a society guaranteeing justice, peace and full harmony with creation. Guided by the values of the gospel message, they will seek to participate in setting up structures that promote the widest possible participation. They will seek to strengthen respect for the dignity of all, especially the vulnerable and the weak. They will give priority to the demands of solidarity. But they are conscious that human life is replete with competing forces and that the order and functioning of society are inevitably based on compromises. Within the complex network of modern society, the best possible solutions must be pursued.[28]

To compromise, however, does not mean to accept the circumstances of globalization. Rather, the builders of sustainable communities are called to be creative and diligent in their efforts to distinguish their means and goals from globalization's dominant models.

Israel Batista

Israel Batista outlines one possible strategic approach for those who choose to challenge the realities of globalization, in his 1997 book *Social Movements: Challenges and Perspectives*.[29] Batista argues that, in direct contrast to globalization's preference for human homogeneity, it is in fact only through diversity that any meaningful unity can be achieved. Inviting us to move from what is too often a macro analysis, Batista points out that the strength of social movements is ultimately drawn from personal, individual commitments to particular communities. According to Batista, it is the lack of such commitments which is often at the root of our inability to establish meaningful and effective alliances.[30]

Batista proposes four areas of work for those who seek to build cooperation within and between diverse communities:

Building a Culture of Solidarity: Based on the goal of building power from below while not losing sight of long-term strategies, such work requires that individual communities learn how to create and maintain physical spaces where people from different groups have an opportunity to meaningfully interact with one another.[31]

Promoting a Culture of Life: Local communities must explore how they can most effectively avoid participating in an economic life which does not take into consideration their cultural and religious values. At the same time, such communities must work to identify how they can support their own members in becoming local economic leaders.[32]

Making National and International Actors Accountable: Globalization has brought with it a profound sense of powerlessness for many communities and individuals, who feel their futures are being decided by unelected and unknown decision makers. In a parallel development, however, grass roots movements and groups are increasingly able to use globalized channels of communication to effectively organize together against the proponents of unsustainability.[33]

Human Promotion: The most important investments must be made in people. Human promotion is concerned with identifying what it takes to help people develop their capacity to participate in social, political and economic decisions and to work creatively towards the future. To work for human promotion is thus to identify the means of breaking down the barriers between individuals and communities and a knowledge of technology, management, training and education. Human promotion must also include honoring a person's capacity to dream, wish, resist and hope in the midst of struggle.[34]

Tony Addy

As Batista has noted, building sustainable social movements clearly involves building alliances across boundaries of difference. Yet alliances cannot be forged in the absence of clearly identifying issues and concerns which cut across traditional social, racial, religious and economic divisions. In his text, *The Globalising Economy: New Risks – New Challenges – New Alliances*, Tony Addy points to the issue of debt burden as one critical challenge which invites a new level of cooperative response.[35] Addy observes that the ideology of globalization "obscures the reality that poverty is not something 'natural' but (is, in fact) the product of a power relationship".[36] Thus, as more communities are able to see a connection between their own specific circumstances and the reality of the debt crisis, opportunities increase for making meaningful connections between different groups at the grassroots level.

Making connections between different peoples and circumstances is essential to building sustainable communities. Yet as Addy notes, meaningful and lasting alliances can only be built by employing a variety of strategies which recognize the specific circumstances, beliefs and languages of individual communities. The debt crisis, observes Addy, provides a clear example of why a homogeneous response to globalization will never succeed.

> [We must] recognise the variations in regional experiences of the impact of debt and the financial system, the different discourses and concepts, and the need to respect a diversity of solutions....including the repaying of "social debt" (a largely Latin American concept) or the making of reparations and restitution (which comes from largely African discourse).[37]

Thus any successful strategy for building sustainable community must hold in tension the specific circumstances and needs of a diverse array of individual groups, while making spaces where people can work together to identify common languages, goals, and a means of mutual accountability. This is arguably the central challenge for those who struggle to realize sustainable communities within the context of a globalized economy.

BUILDING THE COMMUNITIES IN WHICH WE HONESTLY INTEND TO LIVE

While many Christians can recognize and agree with the call to unity advocated by the proponents of sustainable communities, they do so believing that unity is dependent on the maintenance of traditional forms of church and doctrine.[38] At the same time, many advocates of sustainability often insist that any useful analysis must always take place at the international, or global level. In contrast to these perspectives, those who have participated in the WCC's Theology of Life gatherings have found that building community requires a willingness to let go of such assumptions. As Larry Rasmussen has written:

> Now, when suddenly all structures are being called into question, when the rigidities of the system give way to increasing fragmentation, there is a new demand for rebuilding human community, for reconstructing the basic fabric of social and moral life. Our ecumenical reflection, which has focussed for too long on the global situation, has to start again from the everyday lives of people, their struggles and their hopes, their

> powerlessness and their inherent energies for life in communi-
> ty. The prophetic voice of challenge to those in power has to
> be supplemented by the voice of encouragement and sup-
> port for those who sustain the web of life.[39]

What does it mean to live as a contributing member of a sustainable community? How might living in a sustainable community lead one to understand faith, respon-sibility, common ground and inclusivity in a different way? These are some of the many questions posed through the Theology of Life process, which are reflected in the learnings recorded in the document, Working on Theology of Life: A Dossier.

Identifying the qualities of faith which promote sustainable community will inevitably involve an openness to re-reading scripture with new eyes and ears. In her reflection on Genesis 2-4, Brigitte Kahl invited participants of a TOL gathering to re-read a central biblical text with just such a goal, and in so doing laid the bib-lical groundwork for a new understanding of faithfulness to earth:

> Humanity receives its original definition as "servant to the
> earth", being in a clearly dependent and subordinated posi-
> tion, which is expressed in the very naming: Adam (the
> human) of Adama (the earth). God does not create Adama
> for Adam, but the other way round: God creates Adam to
> serve Adama in order to get her green.[40]

Kahl's observation that "humanity is made out of Earth's substance"[41] affirms Rasmussen's explanation of a sustainable faith: turning to God is simultaneously a turning to Earth.[42] At the same time, Kahl emphasizes that the God of Genesis placed the humans in an earthly community which required hard work, but not the type of work globalization favours.

> In the Genesis creation account humanity is created for hard
> labour ....but there aren't any human or divine masters, just
> the earth who needs service. The Biblical paradise is meant to
> work, but (it) is not meant to be a place for slave masters and
> slave work.[43]

How many people assume that the dominant models of community and eco-nomics are based on sound biblical precepts? The "market as God" interpreta-tion of economics clearly benefits from a lack of rigorous biblical exegesis. It is therefore the task of the members of sustainable communities to continually encourage new readings of scripture, by sharing the responsibility and privilege of interpretation with a far wider and more diverse group of people. Sustainable faith requires sustainable exegesis.

If an entire community is to participate in strategizing, exchanging information, or re-reading of text, it can only do so if a common space has been created where everyone can gain entry. Making a space for community has been a major theme that has run though the work of the TOL process. The 1997 Sokoni gathering in Kenya was one effort by the WCC to explore a Southern source of wisdom for creating a common ground. Sokoni, the Swahili word for "marketplace", has traditionally served as place for people to gather as they exchange goods, ideas and the news of the day.[44] By making a Sokoni the setting for a major WCC meeting, many participants who were accustomed to Northern conference formats found their eyes opened to a new way of envisioning a community gathering. While this particular Sokoni was not permanent, the use of this kind of setting raises some central questions for those who aim to build sustainable community, including:

From where will sustainable community's creativity be drawn? Creating a common space for people who are not often inclined or allowed to gather in the same place will require a high degree of creativity. Sustainable communities will therefore inevitably look and feel quite different from what many people are accustomed to.

How will sustainable communities effectively "market" themselves? Sokoni was enticing to its participants. It drew them by its physical form, and by the people within it who offered goods, news and conversation. In a market-driven culture, sustainable communities will have to effectively compete for members with the attractions of a dominant culture that often pulls people apart.

What will give people permission to abandon their old habits and associations? Part of Sokoni's success was found in its ability to encourage people to step away from their accustomed practices and usual conversation partners. For this reason, those who work to build long-term sustainable communities will therefore be asked to face some difficult questions. For example, what would make a Northern businessman willing to risk having a meaningful conversation with a homeless person? What would allow a Southern woman to believe that she would not be exploited by engaging in a face-to-face exchange with a Northerner?

Constructing a common space is central to the task of building sustainable communities. But a space itself is meaningless unless many different people are able to find it, enter and remain. The 1998 Theology of Life Consultation in New York grappled with the difficulties of remaining in a common space.[45] Through their experiences, members of the Consultation identified many of the challenges the ecumenical movement and all sincere advocates of sustainability will have to face, including:

The Need to Decolonize Our Minds: Community cannot be built on language or images which insist on a White God, the Northern way of understanding justice, or an unwillingness to find wisdom in indigenous, local culture and experience. For most people of privilege, listening is often a greater contribution than speaking.[46]

Being Open to Conflict: Too often, gatherings which include a diverse member-ship are only made possible by the silence of the marginalized. Transformation does not come without pain and labour. Prioritizing politeness, deference or silence over honesty and anger prevents the formation of authentic relationships. Human relationships of any weight require a space for face-to-face conflict. The task of building inclusive communities which include people from the North and the South, the rich and the poor, women and men, and across the spectrum of race and ethnicity, is not easy or comfortable – *nor should it be*. What makes such encounters uncomfortable is exactly what makes them worth having.

Recognizing the Real Costs of False Unity: In many cases, the ability of the churches, the ecumenical movement and many social institutions to retain unity is based on their willingness to exclude women, racial and ethnic minorities, and the poor from positions of power. This same exclusion is equally applied to les-bian, gay and bi-sexual people. Suicide by lesbian and gay youth and the hate crimes which kill still others can all too often be linked to the homophobia pro-moted by churches and societies on both sides of the North-South split. Many are afraid to raise these issues for fear of dividing their communities, churches or movements. Yet at what cost to people's lives are we preserving our so-called unity?[47]

From among the varied themes of the World Council documents we have exam-ined, some common strategy recommendations emerge. First, any attempt at building sustainability must include an open declaration by the members of a community of the rationale for taking up such a task, and how it is different from the way things are being done. Secondly, the builders of sustainable communi-ties must know as much as they can about their opponents, their track records, their intentions and their points of weakness, in order to bring about a communal plan of action with the best chance of success. Finally, those who intend to build sustainable communities must cultivate a willingness to look within at their own definitions of community, unity and justice while always remaining open to change. While these three strategies comprise a loose blueprint for one approach to building sustainable community, it is clear that each community must choose what will work in its own particular context. Yet for many, particularly in the South, the issue is not how to build sustainable communities, but rather how to preserve and defend those which already exist. It is this work that will be examined in the following chapter.

[1]The World Council of Churches, *Climate Change and the Quest for Sustainable Societies* (Geneva: WCC Publications, 1998).

[2]*Ibid.*, p. 32

[3]*Ibid.*

[4]*Ibid.*

[5]*Ibid.*, p. 33.

[6]*Ibid.*

[7]*Ibid.*, p. 35.

[8]*Ibid.*

[9]*Ibid.*

[10]*Ibid.*

[11]*Ibid.*

[12]*Ibid.*

[13]*Ibid.*

[14]*Ibid.*

[15]*Ibid.*, p. 36

[16]For more on this topic, see the statement made by the WCC delegation to the Fifth UN Commission on Sustainable Development (CSD5), entitled "Building a Just and Moral Economy for Sustainable Communities", in *Report to the WCC Member Churches Concerning the UN Earth Summit +5 Review Process*, 1997, p. 41.

[17]Dickinson, Richard, *Economic Globalization: Deepening Challenge for Christians* (Geneva: WCC Publications, 1998).

[18]*Ibid.*, p. 5.

[19]*Ibid.*, p. 6

[20]*Ibid.*

[21]*Ibid.*

[22]*Ibid.*, pp. 6-7, 11.

[23]*Ibid.*, p. 8.

[24]*Ibid.*, p. 3.

[25]de Santa Ana, Julio, ed., *Sustainability and Globalization* (Geneva: WCC Publications, 1998), p. 14. It is important to note that de Santa Ana follows this statement by noting that "we must be reminded that globalization is a complex process, and (therefore) both comprehensive endorsement or blanket rejection of it is morally and conceptually simplistic." *Ibid.*

[26]*Ibid.*, p. 16.

[27]*Ibid.*, p. 19.

[28]*Ibid.*, p. 21.

[29]Batista, Israel, ed., "Social Movements: A Personal Testimony," *Social Movements: Challenges and Perspectives* (Geneva: WCC Publications, 1997).

[30]*Ibid.*, p. 2.

[31]*Ibid.*, p. 5.

[32]*Ibid.*, p. 6.

[33]*Ibid.*, pp. 6-7.

[34]*Ibid.*, p. 7.

[35]Addy, Tony, ed., *The Globalising Economy: New Risks – New Challenges – New Alliance* (Geneva: WCC Publications, 1998).

[36]*Ibid.*, p. 5.

[37]*Ibid.*, p. 7.

[38]Rasmussen, Larry, "Theology of Life and Ecumenical Ethics," *Working on Theology of Life: A Dossier* (Geneva: WCC Publications, 1998), p. 13.

[39]*Ibid.*

[40]Kahl, Brigitta, "Fratricide and Ecocide: Genesis 2-4" in *Working on Theology of Life: A Dossier*, (Geneva: WCC Publications, 1998), p. 39.

[41]*Ibid.*

[42]Rasmussen, Larry, *Earth Community, Earth Ethics* (Maryknoll, NY: Orbis Books, 1996), p. 277.

[43]Kahl, Brigitta, "Fratricide and Ecocide: Genesis 2-4", p. 39.

[44]"The Sokoni, A Story" in *Working on Theology of Life*, p. 101.

[45]"Theology of Life Consultation at Union Theological Seminary" in *Working on Theology of Life*, pp. 118-128.

[46]These points are drawn from a presentation made by Adam Clark, of Union Theological Seminary, *ibid.*, pp. 121-122.

[47]These points are drawn from a presentation made by Janet Parker, of Union Theological Seminary, *ibid.*, p. 122.

V.

FIGHTING FOR SUSTAINABLE COMMUNITIES: THE WORLD COUNCIL OF CHURCHES AND THE WORK AHEAD

> Five hundred years ago, it was enough to be a non-christian culture to lose all claims and rights. Five hundred years after Columbus, it is enough to be a non-Western culture with a distinctive worldview and diverse knowledge systems to lose all claims and rights.[1]
>
> Vandana Shiva

While many members of the geographic and economic North struggle to make their communities sustainable for the first time, many others, especially in the South, are fighting to preserve control over their own far more sustainable ways of life. The documents produced by the World Council which engage issues of sustainability are helpful on a number of levels; they disseminate critical information, provoke conversation, offer new vocabulary and interpretation, invite needed reflection, and challenge the churches to a higher standard of conduct. Yet for many struggling communities, it is not a new framework of analysis or vocabulary that is needed, but rather an immediate strategy for survival.

It is clear that the struggle for sustainability is one which must be waged by different communities in different contexts by means which are locally and culturally appropriate. However, despite all the variables and particulars associated with any one community's experience and circumstances, there is one common quality found in all successful efforts to build and preserve sustainable communities: the applied use of creativity. The following is an example of how one group creatively fought against tremendous adversity in the name of survival and sustainability.

LESSONS FROM CHIAPAS: THE ZAPATISTAS AND THE CONDUCT OF SOCIAL NETWAR

In January of 1994 in the southern Mexican state of Chiapas, the international community witnessed the emergence of a new method of countering the dominant development model. The rebellion which took place was noteworthy in several ways. First, the majority of the rebels who gathered under the Zapatista banner came from Mexico's indigenous peoples. Secondly, the Zapatistas' aim was not to overthrow the Mexican government, but rather to reclaim their communities, which were being destroyed by modern methods of development.[2]

> (The Zapatista Movement) did not call upon the government for cheaper food, more jobs, more health care, and more education. Rather than trying to find its niche in Mexico's efforts to solve its problems by strengthening its role in a global economy organized around the needs of consumer society, (the Zapatistas) sought to order (their) own world around the organic needs of community. (The rebellion) was not a revolt in response to a lack of development but a response (to the fact) that Chiapas was being "developed to death."[3]

Given these aims, it is not surprising that the initial uprising coincided with the enactment of the North American Free Trade Agreement (NAFTA), whose terms favored only a small portion of the Mexican population.[4] Finally, the Zapatista uprising distinguished itself through its highly creative tactics, which offer valuable lessons to those fighting for sustainable community.

At first glance, the Zapatista uprising began rather conventionally, through the use of armed force to gain control over four small towns. The Mexican government responded as expected and dispatched 12,000 troops to the region. The Zapatistas, who retreated from the towns and were pursued by the military, engaged the army until twelve days later when the Mexican government, with domestic and international opinion strongly against the conflict, unilaterally declared a cease-fire and began negotiations with the Zapatistas.[5] Yet what would have garnered such an enormous domestic and international outcry in the short span of twelve days, one large enough to force the Mexican government to negotiate with a group of marginalized Indigenous people? In the answer to this question lies the reason why the Zapatistas' tactics merit a closer look.

The Zapatista uprising began with the use of armed conflict, but it quickly evolved into a far more effective non-violent rebellion, creatively engaging thousands of people who came from within and outside of Mexico to provide support. The means of the Zapatistas' success involved a method of organization which used some of the most modern forms of communication available. At the same time, the Zapatistas organized themselves and their supporters in new ways which made them more difficult to infiltrate, divide and destroy.

Although the Zapatistas were ultimately unable to gain control of the region they occupy, their tactics have served to keep their movement, and many of the people they seek to protect, alive. Further, the successes the Zapatistas have enjoyed in the face of overwhelming odds have left governments and corporations scrambling to identify ways to counter their tactics. The United States government is first among those who found the events in Chiapas alarming, so much so that the U.S. Army commissioned a study on the tactics of the Zapatistas and the manner in which they could be effectively undermined. The study, written by the RAND corporation and entitled *The Zapatista Social Netwar in Mexico*, is a fascinating document. Yet while the document is clearly useful to those who wish to counter similar rebellions, it is equally useful to those who would like to employ some or all of the Zapatistas' tactics.

THE CONDUCT OF SOCIAL NETWAR

The researchers at RAND concluded that the best way to describe the actions of the Zapatistas was in terms of human and technological networks. The networks employed by the Zapatistas involved people within and outside of Mexico using the internet, telephones and other means of communication to quickly let the world know what was happening in Chiapas. The Zapatistas used these same networks to strategize among themselves, as well as to organize non-governmental support and action for the movement. NGO support included gathering people outside of Mexico to come to Chiapas and act as witnesses to the events. In many cases, the presence and reports of such witnesses prevented atrocities by the Mexican military and bought the Zapatistas time for more strategizing and action. The network constructed by the Zapatistas and their allies played one other crucial role: it allowed the Zapatistas to shape public perception of events before the Mexican or U.S. governments had a chance to offer their own interpretations. Many news organizations subsequently based their reports on information supplied by the Zapatistas themselves, leaving the Mexican and U.S. governments to play catch-up.

One can see how the combination of such networking tactics could be seen as a modern means of warfare. This is precisely the thesis of the RAND researchers and those who commissioned their work. But what exactly is the structure of the network employed by the Zapatistas? According to *The Zapatista Social Netwar*, an effective network is a group which is organized in a non-centralized and non-hierarchical way.[6] In other words, a sustainable network does not have a traditional chain of command, nor one leader upon which the structure of the group is centred. An obvious leader can be easily identified by his or her opponents, and the elimination of *the* leader means the quick debilitation of the group. The Zapatistas' experience has taught that human and computer networks can thrive using this model, which the RAND writers refer to as "an all-channel network".[7] Ideally, the all-channel network means that everyone can communicate with everyone all the time, rather than through a linear chain of command or via the approval of a centralized authority. In the all-channel network, plans can be made more quickly and organically in response to breaking events, and different people or groups can work in their own fields of expertise while others perform different tasks, which draw on their particular strengths. For example, while one NGO coordinates the arrival of a new group of observers to the sight of a conflict, another NGO can be organizing the press release describing why the observers are especially necessary at this time.[8] Clearly, any community which can effectively concentrate on more than one task simultaneously increases its effectiveness. At the same time, any community which knows how to honor and lift up the expertise and leadership of the widest number of its members stands a much better chance of remaining physically and spiritually intact. For these reasons and many more, it can be argued that the Zapatistas' network model is one very useful means of realizing the non-hierarchical, non-centralized approach to defining organization, power and responsibility that sustainable communities will require.

While the Zapatistas' tactics might appear impossible to replicate at first glance, social and technological developments are placing the network within easy reach of an expanding number of communities. Building a network clearly requires establishing ties to NGOs, preferably inside and outside of the region/country in question. The increased presence of local NGOs world-wide makes this task easier with each passing year, as local NGOs can often provide communication links to transnational NGOs. The growth of NGOs has also included the emergence of organizations that exist to supply computer training and network access to communities on every continent who have had no previous means to acquire such services. One such organization is the Association for Progressive Communications, a non-profit global organization of computer networks and support systems with multiple affiliates.[9] The APC provides computer conferencing, e-mail, and the means for fax-writing campaigns to those who want to go on-line.[10]

Logic dictates that netwar cannot be effectively waged in all circumstances or by any group. Certain conditions and tactics are recommended. For those with access to a transnational NGO, the RAND study describes the optimal strategies and climate for waging netwar to include the following:

Make Civil Society the Forefront: Work to build a local network of people who are linked to local NGOs, through which transnational NGOs and other groups can eventually be drawn into alliance.[11]

Make Information and "Information Operations" a Key Weapon: Demand freedom of access and information, work to capture media attention, and use all manner of communications technologies available. The battle tends to be largely about information – about who knows what, when, where, how and why. Networks must prioritize placing the faces and voices of local people being affected by the conflict into the public domain before other interests can shape the story.[12]

Work to Develop the Capacity to Rapidly Gather Outside Observers to the Place of Conflict: This is one of the most effective ways to overwhelm a government or other target organization. Such gatherings must be planned as part of a deliberate strategy, and not left to chance.[13]

The Society in Question Should be Relatively Open or Opening Up: The freedom to associate and to exchange information to some extent should be in effect.[14]

The Society in Question Should be in Flux: Netwar is most effective in a country or region which is under political, economic, or other strains which are generating divisive public debate. Societies in flux may be especially vulnerable to netwar if they are governed by old clannish and hierarchical leadership structures, which are having a difficult time adapting to new market and civil society forces.[15]

NGOs Should be Used to Expand the Venue of Conflict: Transnational NGOs and their networks should ideally have sufficient reach that they can not only arouse public opinion, but also lobby their causes in Washington, Brussels, Tokyo and other capitals where critical policy decisions are being made.[16]

A Target Government or Corporation Should Care About Its International Image, and Be Sensitive to Its Disruption: The more a government or corporation cares about presenting to the world a particular image or attracting and maintaining foreign investors, the more vulnerable it may be to a netwar, which jeopardizes its image.[17]

While nation-states, multinational corporations and large organizations have long used the emerging information networks to their own advantage, there is no reason why smaller groups fighting for their survival should not make every effort to avail themselves of the same resources. Transnational ties can now be acquired through a telephone line. While telephone lines are still an unreachable luxury for many of the world's poorest people, the market forces of globalization are, out of their own interests, working hard to change this fact. Creative builders of sustainable communities must always be striving for access to new sources of power and influence. For some, netwar is one possible means to that end.

CONCLUSION: WHO EATS AT OUR TABLE?

The writings referred to in this text cover a wide spectrum of concerns, approaches and recommendations. Yet it would seem that the ability to build and defend sustainable communities depends first and foremost upon whom we are willing to invite to eat and remain at our tables. Any group of people who wish to change their community's relationship to greater creation will very likely have to begin by changing their relationships to one another. This is because no viable network can function without a diverse group of people who have chosen to work together and who recognize each other's inherent value and dignity.

Jesus was not a follower of social convention. He was a leader who broke with expectations, often in the most outrageous ways. At this juncture in Earth's history, sustainable communities are seen by many as a particularly outrageous proposition, as much for what they embrace as for what they reject. For this reason, the builders and defenders of sustainable communities cannot expect to always experience personal comfort or widespread affirmation. In fact, it may well be that building and defending sustainable communities has very little to do with comfort at all.

Larry Rasmussen has written that healing begins in mercy, where God's own strength is tapped. Sustainable communities, he states, are therefore found in entering into the predicaments of those who suffer, for compassion (suffering with) is the passion of life itself.[18] We must therefore ask: what will move individuals to place themselves physically in harm's way on behalf of someone with whom they do not already see themselves as being closely related? What will lift the veil that prevents us from seeing the stranger, or the one whom we call "other", as our neighbour?

The power to build sustainable communities is dependent on the grace of God and the strength and integrity of human connections. Making and maintaining these connections are two of sustainability's greatest challenges. Being committed to one's own survival and liberation is easier than fighting for someone else's. Those who suffer on the cruelest margins must reserve all of their strength to fight for themselves. Yet those who have the spiritual and/or material resources to place themselves within another's circumstances will have to confront and overcome their fear and their prejudice, or the term "sustainable communities" will mean nothing more than a set of well-meaning words.

The vision of sustainable communities embraces an all-channel network that will challenge everyone. In these communities, those who fight for racial justice cannot limit their struggles to the liberation of men. In these communities, those who fight for the liberation of women cannot limit their efforts to women of their own race. In these communities, those who fight for the rights of non-human creation cannot expect to be supported if they fail to also demonstrate an equal commitment to the liberation of *all* of their human neighbours.

For many, Jesus distinguished himself more by his choice of eating companions than by any words he uttered. He ate with both the offensive rich and the repellent poor. He ate with tax collectors and with those thought to be ritually unclean. Jesus even managed to eat with those who had been shunned by the marginalized, as well as those rejected by the dominant groups. No doubt, Jesus' choices frightened many of his contemporaries. Later, when he was proclaimed the Messiah, the memory of these same choices instilled an even deeper fear.

Whom are we willing to invite to remain at our table and share our food? How much power are those of us who possess power willing to give up? Jesus' willingness to defy expectations and cross boundaries is a model which has something to say to every group at every level. In building and defending sustainability, each community in its own location must interpret together Jesus' table lessons for itself, and do so with creativity and courage. This is the foundation of sustainable community.

In my own church community, a parishioner wrote the liturgy which we as a congregation recite together every Sunday as our invitation to the offering.[19] From my own context, I can think of no better way of describing my understanding of Jesus' definition of sustainable communities than through her words:

One: In this world, someone has too much.

All: Someone has barely enough, someone has nothing at all.

One: When we share our commitment and financial support, we act on the imagination of Jesus.

All: Who sees enough bread to go around, enough courage to speak the truth, and enough love to overcome all things.

One: O God, to those of us who have hunger, give bread. And to those of us who have bread, give the hunger for justice.

All: When the 5,000 were hungry, the disciples came to Jesus and said: "Send the people away, so they may get something to eat."

One: Jesus answered: "You give them something to eat."

(The plate is passed, and then these words are read)

One: And the people reached in their pockets and pulled out the bread and fishes and shared them, and there was abundance for all, and even more.

All: AMEN

COME, HOLY SPIRIT, RENEW THE WHOLE CREATION

How will we best develop our ability to listen to the most outrageous of Jesus' proposals and envision ourselves not simply as members of an audience, but rather as communities of people who willingly heed a call to action? Where will the imagination come from which will allow us to see beyond the present time in which the neo-liberal economic model seems to have triumphed? How can we come to see ourselves and our communities as having worldly powers which we are repeatedly told we do not possess? Come, Holy Spirit, and renew the whole Creation. Come, Holy Spirit, and renew our sense of imagination, strength and creativity. Come, Holy Spirit, and renew and expand our sense of justice and thus our willingness to act on the teachings of Jesus. Come, Holy Spirit, you speaker of all languages, and teach us how we can more fully and intelligently communicate across boundaries of difference - and even with those who wish to cut off communication!

All: When the 5,000 were hungry, the disciples came to Jesus and said: "Send the people away, so they may get something to eat."

One: Jesus answered: *"You give them something to eat"*.
(So) the people reached into their pockets and pulled out the bread and the fishes and shared them, and there was abundance for all, and even more.

Sustainable communities are not miracles which will emerge from thin air. Rather, sustainable communities are born out of the work and faith of communities who have chosen to defy social, cultural, economic and religious conventions, by drawing on strengths which are not exclusively their own. Time and time again, it has been the Spirit who has pushed us beyond the limits of our own imagination, and it has been the Spirit who has given us the strength to abandon convention. We must therefore never hesitate to consciously and deliberately invite the Spirit to be our guide in all of our actions. For despite any information to the contrary, the market is not God; God is God. And it is through the Spirit of God that we are reminded of the truth that only God and *all* of God's creation can determine what can and cannot be changed.

Come, Holy Spirit, and renew *the whole creation*. Come, Holy Spirit, and open our eyes so that we may see the world and ourselves more as you do. Come, Holy Spirit, and guide our actions. Come, Holy Spirit, *and be with us now*.

[1]Shiva, Vandana, *Biopiracy: The Plunder of Nature and Knowledge* (Boston, MA: South End Press, 1997), p.4.

[2]The Zapatistas' original press conference made the following statements, including : 1. A call for respect for indigenous peoples; 2. A call for abrogation of the North American Free Trade Agreement; 3. A denial that it wanted to seize power; 4. A call to Mexican Civil Society to join it in struggling for social, economic, and political change without necessarily taking up arms; 5. A call for the Red Cross and international human rights groups to come to Chiapas and monitor the conflict. For more details, see Ronfeldt, David, John Arquilla, Graham E. Fuller, Melissa Fuller, *The Zapatista Social Netwar in Mexico* (Santa Monica, CA: Rand, 1998), p. 2.

[3]Rasmussen, Larry, *Earth Community, Earth Ethics* (Maryknoll, NY: Orbis Books, 1996), p. 129.

[4]Chomsky, Noam, *Profit Over People: Neoliberalism and the Global Order* (New York: Seven Stories Press, 1999), p. 122.

[5]Ronfeldt, David et al., *The Zapatista Social Netwar in Mexico* (Santa Monica, CA: Rand, 1998), p. 133.

[6]*Ibid.*, p. 9.

[7]*Ibid.*, p. 11.

[8]This description of a network provides an introduction to the concept, but by no means is a substitute for the RAND text. For a full description, see Ronfeldt, David, et al., *The Zapatista Social Netwar in Mexico.*

[9]See Appendix II for a listing of the APC's international affiliates, their contact numbers and addresses.

[10]*Ibid.*, p. 55.

[11]The Zapatista Social Netwar in Mexico, p. 119.

[12]*Ibid.*, p. 119.

[13]*Ibid.*, pp. 119-120.

[14]*Ibid.*, p. 121.

[15]*Ibid.*

[16]*Ibid.*

[17]*Ibid.*

[18]Rasmussen, Larry, *Earth Community, Earth Ethics* (Maryknoll, NY: Orbis, 1996), pp. 261, 284-285.

[19]Written by Gabriella Lettini, a Waldensian minister and a member of Jan Hus Presbyterian Church, New York, New York, 1998.

APPENDIX I:
THE WCC'S WORKING DEFINITION OF THE ELEMENTS OF SUSTAINABLE DEVELOPMENT

Sustainable/Sustainability

1. Population Stability
2. Renewable Resources
3. Economic Continuity
4. Technological Innovation
5. Limits on Material Wealth
6. Human Cooperation
7. Human Community
8. The Ecosphere
9. Requires Physical Effort
10. Requires Spiritual Effort
11. Recognizes Limitations
12. Recognizes Strengths
13. Human Communities
14. Human Communities Understanding Their Responsibility to the Greater Creation
15. Human Communities Understanding Their Dependence Upon the Greater Creation
16. Human Communities Recognizing that an Absence of Justice Will Ensure an Absence of Sustainability
17. Human Communities Recognizing that They Are Not the Centre of Creation, but Are Instead Important Members of a Greater Web of Life
18. Confession and Repentance by Those Who Have Colluded in Creation's Destruction
19. Requires Faith and Hope

Development

1. Requires Community
2. Involves Social Transformation
3. Does not Marginalize the Human and Non-Human Members of Creation
4. Requires Distinguishing between the Excesses of the North and the Basic Necessities of the South
5. Yields to Precautionary Actions to Prevent Environmental Degradation
6. Does not Make Production of Revenue its Principle Goal
7. Does not Make Jobs, Communities and the Ecosystem Secondary to Maximizing Profit
8. Does Not View the Non-Human World Exclusively in Terms of Its Monetary Value
9. Does Not Discount Values Which Cannot be Expressed in Monetary Terms
10. Recognizes that Humans Exist Within an Ecosystem
11. Promotes a Community Ethic
12. Does Not Engender a Cult of Money
13. Does Not Engender a Cult of Performance
14. Does Not Engender a Cult of Instant Gratification
15. Seeks to Satisfy Basic Human Needs
16. Addresses Material Needs of Creation's Entire Community

Sustainable/Sustainability

20. Requires Greater Humanity to Recognize the Wisdom of Indigenous Peoples

21. Requires Recognizing that the North has Contributed to Creation's Destruction More than the South

22. Requires New Relationships Between Humans, Between Humans and Non-Humans And Between Humans and Their God

Development

17. Addresses Social Needs of Creation's Entire Community

18. Addresses Spiritual Needs of Creation's Entire Community

APPENDIX II:
COMMUNICATIONS RESOURCES

The Association for Progressive Communications (APC) is the world's most extensive network of Internet providers dedicated to serving non-governmental organizations (NGOs) and citizen activists. The APC is a non-profit association of member networks working together to provide online organizing and collaboration tools and skills for civil society. The following is a list of the APC's current principal members, which includes e-mail addresses, telephone numbers, mailing addresses and web site locations. For more information, contact the APC at APC Secretariat, Presidio Building 1012, Torney Avenue P. O. Box 29904, San Francisco, CA 94129, tel. (based in Toronto, Canada) +1 416 516-8138, fax +1 416 516-0131, e-mail: apcadmin@apc.org, or contact their web site: http://www.apc.org/

Inquiries can also be made to the APC member closest to you:

ARGENTINA
Wamani
Talcahuano 325-3F
1013 Buenos Aires
Argentina
Tel: +54 1 382 6842
Fax: +54 1 382 9342
E-mail: apoyo@wamani.apc.org
Website: http://www.wamani.apc.org

AUSTRALIA
Community Communication Online (c2o)
PO Box 304
Richmond 3121
Australia
Tel: +61 3 9486 9764
Fax: +61 3 9486 9765
E-mail: info@c2o.org
Website: http://www.c2o.org

BULGARIA
BlueLink Information Network
Morava House
Pozitano 114 - B, Floor 4
Sofia 1303
Bulgaria
Tel: +359 2 920-1547/292-2151
Fax: +359 2 217623
E-mail: office@bluelink.net
Website: http://www.bluelink.net

CANADA
Web Networks
401 Richmond Street West
Suite 384
Toronto, Ontario M5V 3A8
Canada
Tel: +1 416 596 0212
Fax: +1 416 596 1374
E-mail: outreach@web.net
Website: http://www.web.ca & http://community.web.net

COLUMBIA
Colnodo
Avenida 39 No. 14-75
Santafe de Bogota, DF
Colombia
Tel: +57 1 338 1277
Fax: +57 1 232 4246
E-mail: soporte@colnodo.apc.org
Website: http://www.colnodo.apc.org

CZECH REPUBLIC
Econnect
Ceskomalinska 23
160 00, Praha 6
Czech Republic
Tel: +420 2 2431 1780
Fax: +420 2 2431 7892
E-mail: support@ecn.cz
Website: http://www.ecn.cz

ECUADOR
INTERCOM Nodo Ecuanex
Av. Amazonas 258 y Jorge Washington, piso 4
Quito, Ecuador
Tel: +5932 507158 + 5932 507159
Fax: +5932 507158 + 5932 507159
E-mail: intercom@ecuanex.net.ec
Website: http://www.ecuanex.net.ec/

GERMANY
ComLink
Im Moore 26, D-30167
Hannover, Germany
Tel: +49 511 161 7811
Fax: +49 511 165 2611
E-mail: support@comlink.org
Website: http://www.comlink.org

HUNGARY
GreenSpider
2600 Vac,
Ilona u. 3.
Hungary
Tel: +36 27 305769
Fax: +36 27 304483
E-mail: support@zpok.hu
Website: http://www.zpok.hu

JAPAN
JCA-NET
3-21 Nishiki-cho, Kanda, Chiyoda-ku,
Tokyo, Japan
Tel: +81 3 3291 2875
Fax: +81 3 3291 2876
E-mail: support@jca.ax.apc.org
Website: http://www.jca.ax.apc.org/

MEXICO
LaNeta
Alberto Zamora #126
Col. del Carmen, Coyoacan
04100 Mexico, D.F.
Mexico
Tel: +52 5 554 19 80
Fax: +52 5 554 31 59
E-mail: soporte@laneta.apc.org
Website: http://www.laneta.apc.org

NICARAGUA
Nicarao
Apartado 3516, Iglesia El Carmen
1 cuadra al Norte,
1/2 cuadra al Oeste.
Managua, Nicaragua
Tel: +505 2 225217
Fax:+505 2 2681565
E-mail: ayuda@nicarao.apc.org.ni
Website: http://nicarao.apc.org.ni

ROMANIA
StrawberryNet
4000 Sfantu Gheorghe
P.O. BOX 1-24
str. Korosi Csoma Sandor nr. 6
Romania
Tel: +40 92 224176
Tel/Fax: +40 67 312238
E-mail: support@sbnet.ro
Website: http://www.sbnet.ro

SENEGAL
Enda-Tiers Monde
PO Box 3370
Dakar
Senegal
Tel: +221 823 5772
Fax: +221 823 5157/822 2695
E-mail: support@enda.sn
Website: http://www.enda.sn/

SOUTH AFRICA
SANGONeT
P. O. Box 31
13th floor Longsbank Building
187 Bree Street
Johannesburg 2000
South Africa
Tel: +27 11 838 6944
Fax: +27 11 492 1058
E-mail: support@sn.apc.org
Website: http://sn.apc.org

SPAIN
Pangea - Comunicació per a la Cooperació
Jordi Girona Salgado
31 Edifici PL-Pangea
08071-Barcelona
Spain
Tel: +34 93 401 56 64
Fax: +34 93 401 1891
E-mail: suport@pangea.org
Website: http://www.pangea.org

UKRAINE
GLUK (GlasNet Ukraine)
14b Metrologicheskaya str.
Kiev, 252143 Ukraine
Tel: +7 044 266 9481
Fax: +7 044 266 9475
E-mail: support@gluk.apc.org
Website: http://www.gluk.apc.org

UNITED KINGDOM (U.K.)
GreenNet
4th Floor
74-77 White Lion Street
London N1 9PF
U.K.
Tel: +44 207 713 1941
Fax: +44 207 837 5551
E-mail: support@gn.apc.org
Website: http://www.gn.apc.org

UNITED STATES OF AMERICA (U.S.A.)
Institute for Global Communications
Presidio Building 1012, First Floor
Torney Avenue
P.O. Box 29904-0904
San Francisco, CA 94129-0904
United States
Tel: +1 415 561 6100
Fax: +1 415 561 6101
E-mail: igc-info@igc.apc.org
Website: http://www.igc.org

URUGUAY
Chasque
Casilla Correo 1539
Montevideo 11000
Uruguay
Tel: +598 2 409 6192
Fax: +598 2 401 9222
E-mail: apoyo@chasque.apc.org
Website: http://www.chasque.apc.org/

APPENDIX III:

FURTHER READING: FOUNDATIONAL WCC TEXTS ON SUSTAINABILITY

The following texts are drawn from some of the key WCC documents which served to inform the writing of this monograph. While these documents are by no means a definitive collection, they do offer the reader an opportunity to become more familiar with some of the World Council's best known writers who have shaped the discussion on sustainable communities. From Julio de Santa Ana's reflections on sustainability in the context of globalization, to Richard Dickinson's engagement of the Ecumenical Affirmations, to Mercy Oduyoye's definitions of solidarity, the following selections serve to map the work that lies ahead. Yet while the writings which follow represent a worthy foundation for further conversations, the readers of this volume should be asking themselves the following questions: "What is it that is still missing from these writings (including the text which you have just read)?" "Whose voices are being privileged, and which groups have yet to be heard?" and "If the work of sustainable communities is to be fully realized, then what must still be abandoned, and what needs to be embraced?" The concept of sustainable communities by its very definition implies an undertaking which never ceases to move forward and evolve. The reader of any of these texts is therefore encouraged to consider where her or his own voice will enter into the work of building sustainable communities, and how they intend to push the conversation further. DJW

a. Dickinson, Richard, "Rooting Our Concerns in the Ecumenical Affirmations," *Economic Globalization: Deepening Challenge for Christians*, Geneva: Unit III, 1998, pp. 17-35.

b. de Santa Ana, Julio, "Is a Sustainable Society Possible in the Context of Globalization?", *Sustainability and Globalization*, Geneva: WCC Publications, 1998, pp. 1-21.

c. Batista, Israel, "Social Movements: A Personal Testimony," *Social Movements: Globalization, Exclusion*, Geneva: WCC, 1997, pp. 1-7.

d. "Ten Affirmations on Justice, Peace and the Integrity of Creation," *Now is the Time: The Final Document and Other Texts from the World Convocation on Justice, Peace and the Integrity of Creation*, Geneva: WCC, 1990, pp. 11-21.

e. "Chapter 12: Theological Issues," *Climate Change and the Quest for Sustainable Societies*; Geneva: WCC Unit III, January 1998, pp. 38-41.

f. Rasmussen, Larry, "Sustainable Development and Sustainable Community: Divergent Paths," in *Development Assessed: Ecumenical Reflections and Actions on Development*, Geneva: WCC, 1995.

g. Rasmussen, Larry, "Theology of Life and Ecumenical Ethics," *Working on Theology of Life: A Dossier*, Geneva: WCC Unit III, 1998, pp. 12-24.

h. WCC delegation to the Kyoto Summit on Climate Change, "Statement to the High Level Segment of the Third Session of the Conference of the Parties (COP3) to the UN Framework Convention on Climate Change", Kyoto, Japan, December 9, 1997.

i. WCC Delegation to the Fifth Session of the UN Commission on Sustainable Development, "Building a Just and Moral Economy for Sustainable Communities"; April 10, 1997, New York.

j. Oduyoye, Mercy, "The Meaning and Signs of Solidarity," *Who Will Roll the Stone Away? The Ecumenical Decade of the Churches in Solidarity with Women*, Geneva: WCC, 1990, pp. 43-49 .

k. "Together on the Way, Resisting Domination – Affirming Life: the Challenge of Globalization", Eighth Assembly, Harare, Report of the Policy Reference Committee II, 1999. "Together on the Way, 5.3. Globalization", Eighth Assembly, Harare, 1999.

Appendix IIIa.

Dickinson, Richard, 'Rooting Our Concerns in the Ecumenical Affirmations', *Economic Globalization : Deepening Challenge for Christians*; Geneva : Unit III, 1998, 17-35

ROOTING OUR CONCERNS IN THE ECUMENICAL AFFIRMATIONS

Here we are not interested in a theoretical debate about Christian ethics. As there is no single Christian perspective, our views are rooted in the emerging values expressed through the ecumenical churches over the past 30 years. The ecumenical family, represented in the World Council of Churches, has a history of articulating its moral/ethical perspectives on economic and social life. At the heart of our inquiry, then, is an attempt to think and live more ethically and faithfully. Why do we challenge the ideology and practice of economic globalization?

Globalization, led by the neo-liberal ideology, competes directly with the ecumenical vision of a united humanity through which differing communities and peoples live in solidarity with each other. The "oikoumene" indicates the whole inhabited and habitable earth. The Greek root "oikos" refers to a community of the household. Of course, the ancient Greek household was patriarchal, while current ecumenical understanding of the household insists upon equality between women and men. Yet this vision of a household of all God's people is belied by the ongoing destruction of biodiversity and the tensions, anxieties, inequalities which people, especially poor people, experience in today's impersonal world. The breakdown of institutions which gave people a sense of belonging and participating — the family, the church, the face-to-face market, the neighbourhood — is experienced on every side. Because nobody wants to be left out, the pressures to conform to new economic and market realities are enormous.

From its inception, the ecumenical movement, basing its affirmations on Christian traditions, is replete with cautions about economic power. These cautions are today even more cogent and urgent in view of the vastly increased power of economic forces, many beyond the scope of effective government control and intervention. In this statement we draw directly upon the emerging ethical perspectives expressed through the ecumenical family over the past several decades. We refer to official statements of the World Council of Churches, primarily as expressed through the Council's four most recent assemblies, the highest expression of that Movement. In many cases, were we to draw upon the broad and rich ecumenical literature aside from the assemblies themselves, we would find even more explicit and powerful articulations!

In the 1940s J. H. Oldham, one of early ecumenism's most prominent leaders, called upon the churches to affirm together certain "middle axioms", affirmations mid-way between ultimate theological convictions and specific or concrete situations. The ecumenical movement frequently has lifted up certain signposts by which to organize or judge economic life. Here we identify seven main challenges to neo-liberal ideology and its expression in economic globalization.

IDEOLOGICAL CHARACTER OF PREVAILING GLOBALIZATION

A basic proposition of neo-liberal economic thinking is that values, other than productivity, growth and efficiency are not the concern of economists. In the maelstrom of millions of individual choices, the invisible hand guides the economy toward an optimum realization of people's values. It sees itself as driven by pragmatic rather than ideological considerations. In earlier centuries it was common to talk about economics as "political economy", a tacit recognition that economics is about broader and deeper issues than productivity, growth and efficiency. Increasingly during the nineteenth century, economics intentionally tried to become de-linked from politics, and claimed a sphere of scientific analysis of its own. Yet every economic theory, including neo-liberalism, has its own assumptions and values, explicit or behind the scenes. As argued above, neo-liberalism operates with an ideology that closely resembles an idolatry — all the more dangerous because hidden or minimized by its proponents.

The ecumenical family rejects this claim to value neutrality. Far from being essentially neutral and valueless, economic globalization is a potent expression and conveyor of values. The ecumenical family sees economic globalization as an institutional expression of a powerful ideology — a system of beliefs and practices, although claimed by its proponents to be universal, that reflects a particular web of values dominated by Western societies. Its values are Western, not Christian. This view puts emphasis on individuals rather than communities; on material well-being as distinguished from holistic health, on humankind as distinct from the wholeness of creation; on the invisible hand behind market forces rather than the human exercise of responsible judgment and freedom, on the elite as harbingers of social progress; on scientific rationalism as the core interpretative principle of human history. Rather than being universal, this web of assumptions and assertions is a belief system rejected by, or at least deeply questioned by, vast numbers of people, especially those from more traditional and less industrialized societies. One author contends that what we need is not so much the "wealth of nations" (Adam Smith), but the "health of nations". (Carol Johnston, The Wealth or Health of Nations?)

Already, in 1948 at the Amsterdam Assembly, it was argued that justice was a desideratum in assessing both political and economic life. Both capitalism and communism, as economic and political systems were soundly judged. The Evanston Assembly enunciated the doctrine of a "responsible society", whose main tenet was that a political or economic order can be just only if those people most affected by it have the right and power to influence and even change it. But today, even the state, which is charged with protecting and enlarging the people's welfare, has reduced influence over the globalization juggernaut. The World Bank's World Development Report, 1997, makes this same point.

The WCC's Canberra Assembly (1992) graphically captures the reality. "What we need, therefore, is first of all a new concept of value, based not on money and exchange, but rather on sustainability and use. Humankind has failed to distinguish between growth and development. Growth for growth's sake is the strategy of the cancer cell. It ultimately results in degradation and death. Development — like the strategy of an embryo — is getting the right things in the right place at the right time and in the right relationships."[9]

"He has shown strength with his arm, he has scattered the proud in the imagination of their hearts, he has put down the mighty from their thrones, and exalted those of low degree." (Luke 1: 51ff) "Be not afraid when one becomes rich, when the glory of his house increases. For when he dies he will carry nothing away; his glory will not go down with him. Though while he lives, he counts himself happy, and though a man gets praise when he does well for himself, man cannot abide in his pomp, he is like the beasts that perish."(Psalm 49:16 ff) "No one can serve two masters; for either he will hate the one and love the other, or he will be devoted to the one and despise the other. You cannot serve God and mammon." (Matthew 6:24) "For the love of money is the root of all evils." (I Timothy 6:10)

PRACTICAL MATERIALISM

Globalization is driven by values which are basically materialistic rather than holistic. As the Canberra Assembly noted, "acquisitive materialism has developed into the dominant ideology of our day"[10]. Meeting basic human needs is, of course, critically important; three-quarters to four-fifths of the world are crying out for even such basic needs to be met, and they could be met if the world would only pay attention. It would be hypocritical to suggest that because being human requires more than material needs, Christians should too quickly leap over issues of basic needs and dwell only on "spiritual" matters. Indeed, meeting basic material needs is a spiritual matter.

Nevertheless, to reduce humankind to homo economicus would be a travesty. The Nairobi Assembly in 1975 made this very clear. "Being implies having. But there exists in humanity a fatal tendency to let having gain the rule over being, to be trapped by the things we possess, to think and believe that having is more fundamental in life. Thus, having becomes pathological and demonic. The corruption of excessive having is consumerism. Its consequent productive processes throw up enormously powerful institutions which now have global impact."[11] "We are spiritual beings. It is the despiritualizing impact of the process which dismays us."[12]

"Man shall not live by bread alone, but by every word that proceeds from the mouth of God." (Matthew 4:4) "Give us this day our daily bread." (Matthew 6:11) "Therefore, do not be anxious saying, 'what shall we eat?' or 'what shall we drink?' or 'what shall we wear?' But seek first his kingdom and his righteousness, and all these things will be yours as well." (Matthew 6:31-33)

CONCENTRATION OF POWER

Globalization concentrates power. No era has seen a greater movement toward corporate mergers; no period in history has witnessed as great a steady, seemingly unstoppable, drive for monopolistic power. The inner logic of capitalism is competitiveness; it demands controlling or exterminating actual or possible competitors; in a global economy which makes space and boundaries irrelevant competitiveness requires giantism.

Economic Darwinism postulates the survival of the fittest. In 1997, in the USA, the pace of corporate mergers had more than doubled from five years earlier, 1992. Instead of under 5,000 "deals" in 1992, 1997 saw 11,000 deals. The money involved in such deals was $500 billion in 1992, while in 1997 it leaped to $1.1 trillion. Prospects for 1998 maintain the same pace. (New York Times, p. BU9, August 2, 1998) Little fish get swallowed up; today, even big fish do too. True believers claim that such competitiveness increases productivity, efficiency and growth — a bigger pie. But competitiveness wreaks havoc on the poor.

Ecumenical literature specifies three main problems with concentration of power. It underestimates the importance of cooperation, mutuality and solidarity in the human community. Indeed, human communities owe far more to collaboration than to competitiveness. Humans are fully persons, not as isolated monads, but as people in community. Second, concentrations of power are toxic for those who exercise such power. Wealth and power mask real need, not only to others but to the self (or corporation).

Third, concentration of power, perhaps categorically, creates or exacerbates disparities between haves and have-nots. The Nairobi Assembly described the "free market" system as having an "in-built exploitative tendency"[13], and in another place referred to the "innate exploitative patterns"[14]. "Transnational corporations represent a concentration of economic and technological power in the hands of a few. These corporations claim to bring capital and technology to the countries where they operate and thereby to create employment and income. But, essentially, their aim is to take advantage of the cheap labour that is available and to draw out profits from them, making use of the immense control they exercise over world trade and prices."[15]

Seventeen years later Canberra picked up the same theme. "Power elites concentrate wealth for the control of political and economic institutions. A special manifestation of injustice is the prevailing international economic order. It has institutionalized domination by Northern economies. Handled mainly through transnational corporations, the economic order subordinates and renders dependent the Southern economies. In sum, economic interests, military might, technological knowledge and international alliances form a constellation of forces arrayed against the dignity of life in the world. The consequences are formidable: immense human suffering, degradation and death."[16]

"Woe to those who join house to house, who add field to field, until there is no more room, and you are made to dwell alone in the midst of the land." (Isaiah 5:8) "Do not lay up for yourselves treasures on earth, where moth and rust consume and where thieves break in and steal, but lay up for yourselves treasures in heaven where neither moth nor rust consume and where thieves break in and steal. For where your treasure is, there will your heart be also." (Matthew 6:19ff.)

EXCLUSION

The opposite side of the coin of concentration of power is exclusion. We speak of exclusion rather than "poverty" because, while some poverty is due to the lack of resources, lack of health and education, etc., some poverty is due to an active (not necessarily intentional) process of exclusion and marginalization. While there is no one-for-one correlation of enrichment with impoverishment, it is clear that the poor are made more vulnerable and marginal when the rich become richer. The relationship cannot be denied.

Despite several decades of efforts to improve the condition of the poor — even the poor within rich countries — the evidence is that the gap between rich (the top 5% or 20% of a society) and the poor (the lowest 20%) has widened appreciably. Enrichment in a "free market", whether within one nation or globally, is not a benign process; it pushes large segments of the population to the margins. It excludes them. It is not necessarily that the rich intentionally relegate the poor to the margins, but the structures of the unimpeded market move in this direction.

The ecumenical family has, from the beginning, condemned this exclusion and marginalization. It is a cardinal conviction that as children created in the image of God, called to responsible citizenship and living, all people have a duty and right to participate in shaping the conditions under which they live. All people are called to be subjects of history, not simply the objects of the history of others. If there has been one major achievement in the last three decades, it is the rising consciousness of the poor that they have a right to self-determination.

This ethical argument is pushed still further. It is among the poor, excluded and marginalized that one most frequently finds agents of justice. It is the ecumenical belief, corroborated by Roman Catholic convictions, that God has a preferential option for the poor. That option is not only because the poor need justice, though that is true. Perhaps even more important is that, without romanticizing the poor, the poor have a special receptivity to the prompting of the Holy Spirit because they are less inclined to try to keep society as it is. Neither the upper economic classes nor the middle class have similar incentives.

"Poverty, we are learning, is caused primarily by unjust structures that leave resources and the power to make decisions about the utilization of resources in the hands of a few within nations and among nations. Unjust structures are often the consequence of misdirected goals and values."[17]

As the Canberra Assembly affirmed, "the preferential option for the poor should be the guiding principle for the churches' efforts in the defense of life".[18] The main task of the churches is to be in solidarity with the poor in their struggles for justice and inclusion. The goal is a community inclusive of all people, all sharing in shaping the policies and institutions of their society. "The Spirit challenges us to an active inclusivity. This means a relentless struggle, in which we side with minorities and oppressed peoples."[19]

"Woe to those who decree iniquitous decrees, and the writers who keep writing oppression, to turn aside the needy from justice and to rob the poor of my people of their right, that widows may be their spoil, and that they may make the fatherless their prey!" (Isaiah 10:1-2) "For wicked men are found among my people; they lurk like fowlers lying in wait. They set a trap; they catch men. Like a basket full of birds, their houses are full of treachery; therefore they have become great and rich, they have grown fat and sleek. They know no bounds in deeds of wickedness; they judge not with justice the cause of the fatherless, to make it prosper, and they do not defend the rights of the needy." (Jeremiah 5: 26ff.)

FRAGMENTATION AND ALIENATION

Paradoxically, while globalization integrates many aspects of the world, it also fragments human life and human communities. Individuals and groups experience fragmentation when they are treated as producers or consumers, but not as decision-making citizens. Families experience this fragmentation when labour markets force migrant workers away from their families. Young women and men leaving the village for the city in search of employment find themselves in a strange and fragmenting environment. Groups experience fragmentation and anomie when the old cohering cultural patterns are eroded by alien, often commercial, values. Whole societies experience fragmentation and loss of traditional moorings as the values of Western culture, often (mis)represented in movies and television, invade their whole environment.

This fragmentation is an image of brokenness and alienation. A major task for the churches in such a situation is not only a pastoral task to bind up the psychological wounds of those individuals and groups which have been fragmented, but also to bring words of prophetic judgment on the forces which generate this alienation.

Fragmentation and uprootedness invite anxiety, fear and despair. The global market erases many traditional signposts which give identity and meaning. The speed of changes, coupled with uncertainties for the future, makes many people aliens in their own land. Millions of others, migrant labourers and refugees, are aliens in other lands. Can I learn the skills necessary for a job in this new company? How long will this company be here and can I count on a job five years hence? If we stop growing this basic food crop for local consumption, can I count on sufficient income, over a period of time, from an alternative cash crop for export? In the new global economy, the common labourer is especially vulnerable. This is true for labourers in both the poorer countries, as well as in the more industrialized ones.

Production can be moved from place to place — wherever labour costs are least, if need be. But labour itself is not so readily free to move without numbing uprootedness, anxiety and fear. Labour has become one of the most expendable variables, exposed daily to the vicissitudes of market priorities and forces. In the long run, labour is in competition with other labour, unions and bargaining power are minimal, and compensation for labour is gradually reduced worldwide. Thus, unemployment and under-employment are stark prospects or realities for perhaps 35% of the world's poor.

"The 54 day General Motors strike [USA, 1998] erupted over local issues...but the strike shared a theme with walkouts as far away as Denmark and South Korea. Underlying these strikes and others is labour's push to resist what many economists say is an irresistible force: globalization which opens markets to fierce competition. It's partly a doomed effort to preserve an old way of life that's not preservable." [20]

Paradoxically, the desperate situation of labour may prove to be an Achilles heel for globalization. Resentment and frustration may become socially explosive. Alternatively, other kinds of economies may emerge, such as small scale and local production, with emphasis on locally controlled economies. Perhaps the reduced compensation and purchasing power of the masses, so necessary for the success of global markets, may undermine the system. Those who believe that capitalism is the final stage of history, or economic development, may be deceived.

The ecumenical family is deeply concerned about fragmentation through the imperial processes of economic globalization. "We cannot be liberated if we are divorced from the culture which bred us and which continues to shape and condition us. Many are taught to despise their culture, many are not participants in the shaping of it. We are not romanticizing indigenous culture; it, too, can have elements which enslave and degrade, but we advocate that people be brought to a critical awareness of the strengths and weaknesses of their own culture rather than being disruptively separated from it to serve the purposes of others."[21]

One way to achieve this strengthening of indigenous culture and enhancing people's participation is to foster "civil society". "These non-governmental public organizations which express the interests and concerns of the people" are critically important. "It is in the civil society that the energy of people aimed at greater emancipation and justice emerges."[22] It is a curious fact that the ecumenical movement has not often overtly supported organized labour.

"When the Lord restored the fortunes of Zion, we were like those who dream. Then our mouth was filled with laughter, and our tongue with shouts of joy. The Lord has done great things for us; we are glad." (Psalm 126) "By the waters of Babylon, there we sat down and wept, when we remember Zion. On the willows there we hung up our lyres. How shall we sing the Lord's song in a strange land?" (Psalm 137)

UNSUSTAINABILITY

Since the 1970s there has been a deepening consciousness of ecological limits – limits to available resources to be exploited and limits to the carrying capacity of the earth's ecosystem. In the main, early discussions centered on issues of sustainability. The recognition of limits to growth posed a direct challenge to those who believed that Western life styles and values should be normative for all societies. "Development" and Western style progress were thought to be the wave of the future. But the earth could not sustain six billion people, and more, living like Americans and Europeans.

Economic globalization seems not to have taken that message seriously — to say nothing of the newer understandings of non-human nature as having its own integrity and value not measured as an instrumental value for humankind. On the ideological level, the costs of razing nature are defined away, as "externalities". Actual practice may be even more devastating. Forests, "the lungs of the earth", are slashed or burned. Agribusiness mines the irreplaceable rich top soils of the earth, and toxic fertilizers used to increase production often hasten this process. Fish are imperiled by those heedless of future generations. Mining operations deface the earth. CFCs contribute to gaping holes in the ozone layer. Carbon dioxide emissions from burning fossil fuels are a major factor in global warming. Are these really "externalities"? If today's quality of life is greatly impaired, can we do anything but despair when we imagine our dreams for our children and our children's children?

The external debt of poorer countries aggravates this situation. In order to repay loans, with interest, poorer countries often accept corporate practices that are careless about environmental costs. Although the debt crisis for poorer countries has not made many recent headlines, those debts are still a millstone on the necks of the poor. In 1996 poorer countries in Africa, Asia and Latin America had an external debt to GNP ratio of 37, while those same countries had a debt service to exports ratio of 1923. Those debts must be repaid with commodities, services and products of the poorer countries, yet the prices paid for many commodities continue to deteriorate. The World Bank reports that deterioration continued apace in 1996. Thus, some nations face the prospect of needing to almost double exports to maintain their same income from those commodities.

The ecumenical community is deeply concerned about sustainability and environmental issues. That concern initially grew out of both limits to growth and justice considerations. While these considerations remain a central part of ecumenical thinking, ecumenical discussion has grown to include a greater, theologically-based, concern for all human and non-human nature as under the creative and redemptive purposes of God. Thus, for example, the Council's commitment in the late 1970s to "Justice, Participation and Sustainability", became in the early 1980s a commitment to "Justice, Peace and the Integrity of Creation".

Two passages from assemblies capture the substance of ecumenical reflections. First from 1975: "We call attention to the growing concern over the consequences of modern science-based technological developments with their accompaniment of a deteriorating environment and debased and alienating forms of human communities. This has resulted in a new call to the affluent both to provide basic necessities for all the people of planet Earth, and to modify their own consumption patterns so as to reduce their disproportionate and spiritually destructive drain on earth's resources."[24] No doubt, this somewhat tepid statement hardly touches the entrenched power of corporations to flout these concerns.

By 1991 these environmental concerns were more prominent. "Disrespect for creation and the destruction of creation can only be described as an act of godlessness."[25] "In the institutions of the sabbath, the sabbatical year, and the jubilee year, the Bible has shown us how to reconcile economics and ecology. Effective economics and stewardship of the earth's resources must be seen together. The biblical vision is of an intimate and unbreakable relationship between development, economy and ecology. This vision is dimmed when progress is seen as the production and consumption of more and more material things."[26]

"And God said to them, 'Be fruitful and multiply, and fill the earth and subdue it; and have dominion over the fish of the sea and over the birds of the air, and over every living thing that moves upon the earth.'" (Genesis 1:28) "And the Lord planted the garden in Eden, in the east. Then the Lord took man and put him in the garden of Eden to till it and to keep it." (Genesis 2: 8,15) "And behold, God saw everything that he had made, and behold it was very good." (Genesis 1:31) "We know that the whole creation has been groaning in travail together until now, and not only creation, but we ourselves groan inwardly as we wait for adoption as sons." (Romans 8: 22-23)

CHALLENGE TO STATE AND DEMOCRACY

This is a provocative way to pose the issue, especially for those neo-liberals who believe that globalization ultimately improves the welfare of the poor by linking their economic activity to global markets, by increasing productivity and often jobs, and by improving the prospects for higher material standards of living. What lies just beneath the surface, however, are more sobering realities. One such reality is the progressive freeing of economic forces from political accountability. This happens in several ways. The elite classes, especially in the poorer countries, become more attuned to external economic powers than to internal democratic movements. Citizens in both rich and poor countries experience a growing sense of helplessness to affect or control the economic forces affecting their daily lives. Perhaps most corrosive is the diminishing capacity of states to control the policies and economic forces to which they are subjected. While global economic powers are very powerful, they also seem faceless.

It has been argued that "failed states", like Somalia and the Sudan, are an expression of neo-liberalism on the global scale: insistence on dismantling diverse existing social systems, in an attempt to replace them with a different one alien to those obliged to live it.

Traditionally, Christian political theory has been more preoccupied with inordinate state power. At the same time, it has generally recognized the positive role that nation states can play in reflecting and representing democratic impulses. Traditionally, one of the chief responsibilities of the nation state has been to protect and assure the well-being of the weakest elements in the population. The view that decisions should be made at the "lowest" (most local) level consistent with "getting the job done" (the principle of "subsidiarity"), has been widely endorsed. Reflecting our tragic experiences with totalitarian regimes, during the last 60 years most ecumenical emphasis has been upon the dangers of too much government or too big government which hindered the power of individuals and groups to make their own decisions.

Today, in a time when global economic forces challenge states' ability to set their own internal policies (e.g. pollution standards, structural adjustment programmes) and external trading relationships (e.g. NAFTA, tariffs), the picture has changed considerably. Already a small number of countries and corporations call the tune. When a World Trade Organization, or perhaps a future Multilateral Agreement on Investment, exerts its power, the role of individual states is greatly compromised. It is deplorable that until they were challenged by citizen's groups, the MAI deliberations were pursued behind closed doors and there was no attempt to be democratic. However, all states, including the rich (e.g. nations of the European Economic Community), find it less and less possible to respond to their own internal democratic forces.

Already, in 1948-54, the ecumenical family stressed the right and responsibility of individuals and groups to shape the society of which they were a part. In the

1970's and 1980's the theme of "people's participation" was a central element in the WCC social agenda. Indeed, participation was a crucial element in the "Justice, Participation and Sustainability" trilogy. And in the Canberra Assembly this appeal to democratic participation is spelled out clearly in the endorsement of the notion of civil society. Political forms to shape and direct the nature of societal interactions have always been deemed essential. We anticipate that as the power of economic globalization becomes more and more pervasive, and increasingly visible and vexatious, the ecumenical family will even more explicitly reaffirm the role of healthy political systems to express the will of the people.

As Samuel nears his death, and his sons do not walk in his way, the people of Israel clamor for a king. Reluctant, Samuel calls upon the Lord. "And the Lord said to Samuel, 'hearken to the voice of the people in all they say to you; for they have not rejected you, but they have rejected me. . . .Only, you shall solemnly warn them, and show them the ways of the king who shall reign over them.'" (I Samuel 8: 6ff.) "So David reigned over all Israel; and David administered justice and equity to all his people." (II Samuel 8:15)

WHAT SUSTAINS US?

The promised Reign of God is a reign of justice for those who have been unjustly treated; it is a Reign of compassion for those who have been fragmented, broken and injured; it is a Reign of accountability for those who have wielded power; it is a Reign of inclusion and solidarity for those who have been marginalized and excluded.

To live fully means to live in the promise of the Reign of God. Sometimes the Reign of God seems near at hand, as when the evil system of apartheid is finally overcome, or when a modicum of peace comes to warring religious communities in Ireland. Sometimes the Reign of God seems very far away, as when civil war ignites a people in Rwanda, the Sudan, or in Sri Lanka. In the Exodus from Egypt, the Promised Land was both near and far away. At both times, in all times, we remember God's promises in the practices of Sabbath. On the Sabbath, we rest and give thanks for the earth that God saw and called good, the earth that is the Lord's in all its fullness. On the Sabbath of Sabbaths, the year of the Jubilee, we remember not only the futility of endless doing and producing, but also that all economic activity has to be regulated by higher realities (e.g. debts are canceled, slaves are released, land is rested, property is returned).

Jesus summarized the divine law in this way, "you shall love the Lord your God with all your heart, with all your soul, with all your strength and with all your mind; and you shall love your neighbour as yourself". In response to the lawyer's question, Jesus replies, "do this and you shall live." (Mark 10:28) For Jesus, life was not mere survival. As John says, "He came among us that we may have life and have it abundantly." (John 10:10)

When John's disciples go to ask Jesus whether he is the Messiah, or should they await another, Jesus replies: "Go and tell John what you have seen and heard: the blind receive their sight, the lame walk, lepers are cleansed, and the deaf hear, the dead are raised up, the poor have good news preached to them." (Luke 7:23 ff.)

We acknowledge that in the context of globalization we and our churches do not stand unequivocally with the righteous. We have compromised our own convictions. We repent for the ways the power of new technologies, the lure of having things, the temptations to superiority and power have diverted our attention from our neighbour who suffers. We acknowledge the temptation we have to strive for our own inclusion in a world which has space for a privileged few.

Further, we are called to action coupled with reflection, to reflection coupled with action. The sustained dynamic interaction between actions in solidarity with the poor, on one hand, and critical reflections on the faith dimensions and implications of those actions, on the other, is an integral part of what sustains us as people of faith. At an earlier stage of ecumenical reflections on these matters, it was argued that Christians needed to have "spirituality for combat" (for justice and dignity). Today we are more inclined to talk about "spirituality through combat", recognizing that it is actually through the struggles that we discover as well as affirm our faithfulness.

Lest our confession and repentance be hollow, we are called to discover and restore our solidarity with the excluded ones. We are called to reflect the koinonia of God, we seek to share in a community in which all participate, all are empowered to live with the dignity to which God calls each of us. We are called to strive for mutuality, rejoicing in the gifts and promise of each person. As one member of our group said, we are called to the four "s": spirituality, solidarity, sustainability, and simplicity.

Different cultures, represented in our conversations these five days, have different terms for this promise of community. In Africa a common term is ubuntu. This means that a person is embedded in a community. "I belong; therefore I exist." "I am because you are." In The Philippines this concept is expressed in the term bayaniham. This refers to a pattern of voluntary, cooperative labour and community support. While new technologies extend power and communication across the world, the in-depth, human, communication expressed in these local communities is a reminder of what genuine mutuality is all about.

A CALL TO MUTUAL ACCOUNTABILITY

Having discussed and examined the mechanisms and consequences of economic globalization, we invite:

our churches

the ecumenical movement

people of other living faiths and ideologies

people of goodwill

relevant people in centers for theological learning

relevant institutions and organizations of secular society

to:

- receive and assess this statement in the exploratory spirit with which it has been prepared
- consider its implications for our diverse vocations
- intentionally walk in solidarity with the excluded in their own life situations
- communicate with priestly, prophetic and pastoral wisdom the ethical concerns expressed in this document, in dialogue with leaders and other knowledgeable people in financial sectors, corporations, and international organizations
- help to mobilize financial resources and other resources to continue the work pursued in this paper.

Notes

[9]Canberra Assembly, 1991, Kinnamon, Michael, ed., Signs of the Spirit, Geneva: World Council of Churches, 1991, p.64.

[10]ibid, p.61.

[11]Nairobi Assembly, 1975, Paton, David, ed., Breaking Barriers, Grand Rapids, Michigan: William Eerdmans, 1976, p.134.

[12]ibid.

[13]ibid, p.123.

[14]ibid, p.131.

[15]ibid.

[16]Canberra Assembly, 1991, Kinnamon, Michael, ed., Signs of the Spirit, Geneva: World Council of Churches, 1991, p.64.

[17]Nairobi Assembly, 1975, Paton, David, ed., Breaking Barriers, Grand Rapids, Michigan: William Eerdmans, 1976, p.123.

[18]Canberra Assembly, 1991, Kinnamon, Michael, ed., Signs of the Spirit, Geneva: World Council of Churches, 1991, p.88.

[19]ibid, p.118.

[20]Greenhouse, Steven, "The Relentless March of Labour's True Force," The New York Times, August 2, 1998, p. WK 3.

[21]Nairobi Assembly, 1975, Paton, David, ed., Breaking Barriers, Grand Rapids, Michigan: William Eerdmans, 1976, p.87.

[22]Canberra Assembly, 1991, Kinnamon, Michael, ed., Signs of the Spirit, Geneva: World Council of Churches, 1991, p.78.

[23]World Bank, World Development Report, 1997, p. 276.

[24]Nairobi Assembly, 1975, Paton, David, ed., Breaking Barriers, Grand Rapids, Michigan: William Eerdmans, 1976, p.140.

[25]Canberra Assembly, 1991, Kinnamon, Michael, ed., Signs of the Spirit, Geneva: World Council of Churches, 1991, p.134.

[26]ibid, p.241.

Appendix IIIb.

de Santa Ana, Julio, "Is a Sustainable Society Possible in the Context of Globalization?", *Sustainability and Globalization*; Geneva: WCC, 1998, pp. 1-21.

IS A SUSTAINABLE SOCIETY POSSIBLE IN THE CONTEXT OF GLOBALIZATION?

The ecumenical movement, like the rest of the world, was surprised by the sudden collapse of "socialist" (communist) countries in the last weeks of 1989, and unprepared for the consequences. Although there had been clear signs as early as 1985 that the "socialist" nations in Eastern Europe (and subsequently China and other "socialist" countries) were abandoning some of their ideological rigidity, the complete disintegration of the Eastern European ideological system was unexpected by churches.

The European Ecumenical Assembly on "Peace with Justice", held in Basel in May 1989, had agreed that, in light of the growing openness in relations between East and West, the task of the European churches was primarily "to facilitate dialogue" between the two rival ideological blocs and thus to encourage peaceful coexistence. Six months later, the major ideological conflict which had divided the world and the ecumenical movement for more than forty years was virtually at an end.

During this same period, the World Council of Churches was making final preparations for the world convocation on Justice, Peace and the Integrity of Creation (JPIC), convened in Seoul in March 1990. That meeting showed how difficult it is for churches today to find consensus on relevant responses to the challenges facing societies in different parts of the world, particularly those related to sustainability.

The significance of this momentous political-economic change was further debated at the WCC assembly in Canberra in February 1991. Assembly Section II was less positive about the outcome of the economic-ideological change which had occurred than the WCC central committee had been in March 1990. The assembly report declares:

After the economic system of the so-called "socialist" countries plunged into deep crisis, many hopes were expressed about the system of the free-market economy. But it appeared that the free-market economy is also unable to adjust to the new world economic order without new social and ecological institutions.[1]

Section II also affirmed that "part of our task is the education of people to raise their consciousness about the world economic and political situation in order to provide them with the tools to practise freedom and justice". The WCC was urged to take up this work.

WCC REFLECTION ON THE CHALLENGE OF GLOBALIZATION

The ecumenical reflection called for by the Canberra assembly renewed impetus to work earlier undertaken by the WCC's Advisory Group on Economic Matters (AGEM). In August 1991 the WCC central committee recommended that AGEM undertake a study of the economic issues facing the churches in the new "global" context. In August 1992 a report by this group of economists and theologians, *Christian Faith and the World Economy Today*, was approved by the WCC central committee and commended for study in the churches. Widely distributed in the churches, this study document stimulated new reflection on the Christian approach to global economic issues after the cold war, especially regarding the responsibility of the rich nations.

The report acknowledged that the demise of communism made possible a new "global" approach to issues of social-economic order and justice. It spoke of interlocking and worldwide realities, which require worldwide processes of handling and solving. It may sound somewhat unreal to speak in these terms when the "normal" contexts of thought and action for most people are the smaller units of family, village, tribe, township or region, and where so much power of decision - and of the educational and ideological shaping of decisions - resides in the nation-states whose common forum in the United Nations system is still far from growing into the forerunner of a world government. Yet one of the unmistakable features of our time is that the trend to greater "globalization" seems irreversible. Environmental threats pay no respect to national borders. Neither do diseases such as AIDS or problems such as drug addiction. Global problems must be seen for what they are, however difficult it is to know how to resolve them.[2]

The report listed nine priority issues for ecumenical reflection:

1. **The shocking extent of "absolute poverty"** and of indifference to it "at a time in world history when the conditions necessary to ensure a minimal living standard for all are entirely (if not straightforwardly) within the powers of the world community".

2. **The growing gap between rich and poor** and "the deterioration in relations between the richer nations of 'the North' and the poorer nations of 'the South'".

3. **The global debt crisis** with many nations "trapped in a permanently crippling vise of financial debt, from which there is no prospect of release anywhere in sight".

4. **Threats to the environment** arising out of "environmentally destructive economic developments... fuelled by social, cultural and ideological processes. Certain theological thinking has not remained immune to this and may even have contributed to it."

5. **Land as an economic commodity**, "treated as an object of speculation and reduced to one more possible source of financial profit".

6. **The differing roles of women and men**. Despite some signs of progress, "those whose views count for most in economic matters still undervalue what women are contributing, let alone what they could if their gifts were more adequately released and rewarded. It is estimated that work of all kinds done by women amounts to more than two-thirds of the hours worked overall, though they receive no more than a tiny fraction of the money income paid... In almost every culture the women are 'naturally' expected to take charge of all that requires doing in the household... Although such work is unpaid, it is nonetheless a crucial ingredient in the economy because it holds together the social fabric of society and forms the base for many activities in the economic realm."

7. **Unemployment and under-employment** in nearly every country. "In India or China, where population has long outstripped available land, under-employment is nothing new, though the weight of it rises... In Western European nations, with their understandably proud record of establishing 'welfare states' after the second world war, the combination of recession and the swing to 'free market' ideological policies in the 1980s is biting hard."

8. **Conflict, war and militarization** "The dissolution of the Warsaw Pact released one major tension that has had incalculable economic consequences over the last forty years... The hopes for a sizeable economic & peace dividend' have not yet found much realization... partly no doubt because of the fears of unemployment. The Gulf war and the civil conflicts in the Caucasus and the former Yugoslavia are dismaying signs that new tensions may inspire no less priority to be given to military readiness."

9. **The key role and often hidden power of communication systems.** "Today, new technologies offer possibilities of wider communication and education for all. At the same time their misuse threatens their true purpose... The economic and political control over media deeply influences what many people are able to think and imagine. The misuse of media can spread consumerism, racism, sexism and religious intolerance."

Already in 1975, the fifth assembly of the WCC noted the "new emphasis" being given to "the goal of a sustainable society, where each individual can feel secure that quality of life will be maintained or improved".[3]

In recent years the notion of sustainability has again been the object of ecumenical reflection and debate. The challenge to affirm sustainability has become more dramatic in the context of the accelerated integration of markets made possible by rapid technological changes, especially in the fields of mobility and communications. Can sustainable societies be achieved within the framework of the present project of world trade? How can the challenges of both justice and sustainability be met under the conditions imposed by the trends of globalization? What orientations in the area of social thought and social action will enable Christians and churches to give a relevant witness to Christian faith in our time?

The three consultations organized by the Visser 't Hooft Foundation and the Ecumenical Institute of Bossey have sought to contribute to a deeper understanding of the implications of the term "sustainability" for Christian social ethics. They have focused on "Sustainable Growth" (1993), "Work in Sustainable Societies" (1995) and "Sustainability and Globalization" (1997).

SUSTAINABILITY

The term "sustainability" basically refers to the need for human beings to recognize the limits inherent in creation and to adapt their claims on the future to a course which can be sustained – that is, maintained for an indefinite time.

The basic dilemma which has led to the more and more general use of the term was set forth by an ecumenical conference already in 1974:

> For a short period in recent history some societies cultivated the dream of unlimited wealth, of overcoming poverty, not primarily by sharing wealth but by increasing it so that there would be enough for all. Now we face a sobering return to reality. We begin to perceive that the future will require a husbanding of resources and a reduction of expectations of global economic growth. We do not expect that humanity can live as the most extravagant have been living, and we no longer believe that the spillover of wealth from the top will mean prosperity for all. There may be a divine irony in the fact that the very technological victories which once supported the vision of affluence now - by their contribution to increasing consumption of resources, growing population and pollution – are bringing an end to the dream of a carefree and affluent future.[4]

Through the Brundtland report on environment and development, published in 1987 under the title *Our Common Future*, the term "sustainable development" found wide acceptance. This report spoke of the need for a "development that meets the needs of the present without compromising the ability of future generations to meet their own needs". In the ensuing debate the term has been used in many different ways.

An adequate definition of sustainability must take account of three basic elements:

1. Sustainability implies concern for the well-being of future generations and their right to a fulfilled life. While each generation constructs its own life and alters the face of the earth, no generation should change the quality of the conditions of life on the planet so profoundly as to deprive future generations of major possibilities to build and construct their life and alter the face of the earth in their own right. This means that each generation must take the greatest possible care not to cause irreversible damage. The first Visser 't Hooft consultation in 1993 defined a sustainable society as "one which leaves the world as rich in resources and

opportunities as it inherited... This means that renewable resources are consumed no more rapidly than renewable substitutes can be found, that wastes are discharged at a rate no greater than they can be processed by nature or human devices."[5]

As clear as these principles may be, they are bound to lead to conflicts. How are the rights of future generations to be measured against the claims of the present generation? In practice, the rights of future generations generally take second place. On closer examination, therefore, this principle of responsibility for future generations is much more demanding than it may appear at first.

2. The second consideration concerns justice. The Brundtland report speaks of the common future of humankind and rightly emphasizes that "the essential needs of the world's poor need to be given over-riding priority" in all efforts to preserve the "environment's ability to meet present and future needs". For the churches this consideration is of particular importance. They stand for the cause of justice. To struggle on behalf of the world's poor is an essential part of their witness.

If sustainability must not be achieved at the expense of justice, the pressing question is how justice can be achieved within the planet's limited potential. The diversity of moral judgments reveals the need for more careful assessment of this potential. One of the strengths of the Brundtland report is that it speaks of the problems of environment, poverty and energy as a single connected crisis. But even if it is generally accepted that only development which opens up a future to all nations may justly be termed sustainable, the implications of this principle are rarely recognized. The dangers that threaten the human race are assessed from the point of view of one's own future.

Taking seriously the need for a "common future" represents a particular challenge to industrialized nations, which not only consume a disproportionately high share of resources but also contribute by their life-style to the destruction of the ecological equilibrium in the South. The quest for sustainability thus exposes a new form of exploitation of the South by the North. A new degree of sharing is required.

3. The third consideration concerns the assessment of threats and risks. How do we responsibly evaluate the risks humanity is facing today? Answers differ widely. Often scientists offer estimates and scenarios which demonstrate that solutions are fundamentally possible in many areas. But the countless studies which show

that the agenda of sustainability can in principle be met assume both the will to put these solutions into practice and the ability to set in motion the required political processes, while tending to disregard the unforeseeable character of historical developments. Environmental studies, for example, normally do not refer to the possibility of war and the need for peaceful resolution of conflicts. Often they also overlook the interconnected and mutually reinforcing character of the various threats to the future.

The quest for sustainabilty thus raises the issue of responsible risk assessment. Four considerations are important in this regard: a. The gravity of a risk cannot be judged in isolation. The danger posed by a particular risk grows when a situation is already exposed to other risks. b. Early action is generally less costly than removing damage once it has occurred. Consequently, when the extent of possible damage cannot be predicted or calculated it is sensible to apply the precautionary principle. c. For Christian conscience the issue of possible or probable victims is of decisive importance. It is one thing to accept risk for oneself, quite another to run it for others. Most studies on risk assessment overlook this. Economic and environmental risks will hit humanity differently in different parts of the world. In risk assessment the vulnerability of the weakest countries must be given overriding attention. d. Measures to avoid risks bring costs and disadvantages. How far should present interests or future harm be taken into consideration? In the debate which followed the publication of the Brundtland report there has been much talk about "no regret measures" - protective action that will be economically useful even if the fear caused by the supposed risk should prove to be unfounded. Often the term is used to delay decisions called for by a sober assessment of a risk. Basically, only measures which ensure long-term sustainability will cause no regret. 1. Can sustainability be achieved within the framework of the present economic system? By combining the terms "sustainable" and "development" the Brundtland report seems to assume an affirmative answer. But this cannot be taken for granted. Deeper changes may be required than simple corrections of present trends. The Brundtland report rightly points to the possibility of further technological achievements and expresses the conviction that the exploitation of resources can in principle be drastically reduced by a more efficient social organization. There is no doubt that new perspectives may arise within the present framework. But the question remains whether such modifications will be able to meet the requirements for a sustainable society or whether more fundamental changes in the orientation of society are called for. With this question in mind the consultation has sought to assess the present trend towards a new model of organizing world trade into one global market.

GLOBALIZATION

Although we are living in a period of transition and the ongoing historical situation is far from being crystallized, it is now possible to say that economic globalization is a process which combines several elements. In the first place, it is the contemporary expression of a strong historical trend which created the world economic system through the internationalization of some markets and the transnationalization of economic enterprises. Second, the globalization of markets has been accelerated in recent decades by technological developments, especially in the realm of computer science and communications. Third, a global market, more integrated than ever before, has been shaped for raw materials, manufactured goods, financial and derivative products. As a result, prevailing global trends are expressions of the different ways the market functions. They are based on the accumulation of instruments, especially at the technological level, which have enabled the creation and development of complex economic devices (for example, the world economic system, different markets at the international level and economic tools aiming at the management of both the system and markets). The combination of these elements results in the acceleration of different types of exchanges, creating new burdens for human beings and making it difficult for them to respond to this constant pressure of urgency.

Many world leaders have unambiguously endorsed globalization, arguing that it is the key to global prosperity. Behind this promise of an improvement of economic life lies an implicit hope: that the process of increasing daily productivity of ordinary working people, which has undergirded relative prosperity for the large majority of citizens in the industrialized world, will do the same for all the people of the earth, substantially improving the current global distribution of income and wealth. Firms of all sizes contribute to the gains of both consumers and the labour force, provided they are competitive. In the process of globalization, hundreds of millions of new jobs are being created, though in new sectors and areas, since industries change under competitive pressure (usually the more labour-intensive industries moving out of higher industrialized economies; in developing countries it is the formerly protected industries which suffer most). In addition, the end of the USSR and changes in Eastern Europe have led many to argue that "there is no alternative" to the market system.

But other voices would resoundingly reject this single frame of reference (la pensée unique) as an ideological defence of the great and growing privilege of the wealthy, who benefit so richly from the globalization of life. The promise of globalization is experienced by many in our world as an empty one. Thus it is said that a process which so thoroughly threatens humanity, culture and environment must be rejected.

From the ecumenical perspective, it is clear that the way forward must involve dialogue among different positions and currents of thought, accepting pluralism and the need for constructive cooperation which aims to define actions based on consensus whenever possible.

This diversity of moral judgments reveals the need for more careful assessment of the different dimensions of what is referred to as "globalization". It is evident that the term covers a number of independent but inter-related activities which have been "globalized": finance, communications, trade, power, technology and the ideological conception of the world. Furthermore there is a globalization of problems in health and the natural environment, exemplified by the HIV/AIDS pandemic and the spread of plant and animal life-forms to regions of the world where they upset an historic ecological balance. Cultural exchanges, which enable peoples to share their values and traditions but also create new tensions, are also described in terms of globalization.

Overarching typologies such as this are always problematic. In seeking to clarify our use of the term "globalization", we should be mindful of several factors. First, technology needs to be recognized as not just one of the things that have become "globalized" but as the underlying factor making a globalized world possible and to a large extent defining its character. In fact, the apparent inevitability of much of this ongoing process of technological change further complicates our moral assessment. The process is with us; we cannot return to an earlier era. Christians must evaluate each possibility and discern those developments which favour and those which threaten our fundamental commitment to sustain humanity, culture and the environment.

Second, there are many who accept the prevailing economic system on the basis of empirical considerations while others reject this single frame of reference. There are indeed some positive outcomes of the prevailing process. The technological changes which make possible the integration of markets also contribute to a more human life for many women and men. Unfortunately, there are also destructive elements in this process.

Indeed, to address issues of "globalization" adequately, we should speak in particular terms of international trade or investment or the transfer of technology. Even better, we should speak concretely, for example, of trade in a particular commodity by given firms in various nations, each with its own unique distribution of land ownership, income, wealth and political power. It is only at this level of detail that the defensible and indefensible aspects of the globalization process can be discerned.

Throughout our assessment we are called to use an operational criterion which enables us at least to begin to assess whether a given action or policy sustains humanity, namely, whether it benefits "the least of these who are members of my family" (Matt. 25:40). When any aspect of globalization fails this critical test, a point of resistance has been identified.

TENSIONS BETWEEN SUSTAINABILITY AND GLOBALIZATION

There are several areas in which elements of the process of globalization affect the requirements of sustainability. Without claiming to provide an exhaustive list, we may mention the following:

1. **Ethical tension.** Globalization implies an economically rational behaviour which is rooted in the philosophical tradition of utilitarianism. For many persons, sustainability is an ethical imperative; and they would advance a social and ecological ethic which takes into account not only economic imperatives, but also justice, social responsibility and participation.

2. **Unlimited growth, reasonable human satisfaction and unfair distribution of resources.** Because the world has limited resources, the prevailing economic trend which aims at permanent economic growth - which characterizes the process of globalization - threatens the sustainability of life and future generations. Furthermore, the product of economic growth is unevenly shared, and the gap between the well-off and the poor is widening. Those who aim at sustainability affirm that the rich minority of the world, which profits from the process of globalization, is wasting a great volume of earth's resources and living far above the level of human need. The debate between those who want more economic growth and those who advocate an "economy of enough" is becoming sharper.

3. **Technology and sustaining humanity.** Technology, which can contribute much to the improvement of life, especially when its innovations take account of the vital needs of human beings and the natural and social environment, is also used to destroy jobs and weaken human communities. This particularly applies to the tensions generated by the exploitation of resources of the South by economic powers who have the knowledge and control of these technologies. Furthermore, a technology which may promote life for some (at least according to prevailing, mostly Western patterns of thought) can at the same time be negative for many others. For example, without any consultation with the wider public, powerful economic agents make critical decisions about genetic manipulations that may threaten human life.

4. **Communications and sustaining humanity.** While developments in modern technologies of information broaden people's possibilities for communicating and inter-relating, there is a very strong trend towards the concentration of global information on trade in the hands of a few powerful commercial actors, whose goals are not made clear to the majority of the public. Yet it should be recognized that people's associations, non-governmental organizations and churches are beginning to use the new computer resources to generate and share information that will enable the poor and marginalized to address some of their problems.

5. **Acceleration of the rhythm of human relationships and transactions.** The technological developments on which the process of economic globalization is based enable quicker contact among people than ever before in history. The acceleration of trade requires financial transactions and information about markets which contribute greatly to economic growth. Computer programmes are designed to react almost instantaneously to fluctuations in the market. Trade can also facilitate easier contact among people. But this new phenomenon inherent to the process of globalization also creates a level of stress and anxiety which is difficult to manage; and some are asking whether this situation is human or sustainable.

6. **The influence of production trends and finance.** The necessary inter-relation of places of production in today's world helps to make visible the basic solidarity of human beings. One of the disturbing realities of our time, however, is the dominating power of financial capital. The specific interests of global finance seem to impose their power on nearly every aspect of human life. Although the majority of investments in many financial markets may come from pension funds for employees, civil servants, churches and the like, their managers often behave aggressively; and in the final analysis those most affected are the impoverished,

who find little space in which to exercise human freedom or to seek alternatives to sustain their lives.

7. **Trade and foreign direct investment.** Increased international trade and direct foreign investment hold out the hope that the people of the developing world may participate in the prosperity enjoyed by others. After generations of almost exclusively providing primary products to the industrialized world, the building of factories in developing countries to process those products for export and to manufacture a large variety of goods for both export and domestic consumption has enabled some people to move out of poverty. Others however have become poorer and experience a growing feeling of insecurity; and the fact is that most developing countries are not enjoying these potential benefits of trade and direct foreign investment.

Moreover, the terms of trade regularly worsen for most underprivileged peoples while they improve for some of the wealthy. This significantly reduces any advantages of trade for those most in need while increasing the advantage of those who already have greater advantage. Transnational corporations press governments - especially, though not only, in the developing world - for concessions on taxes, labour regulations and environmental standards by threatening to move elsewhere if they are not granted. Social justice is thus undermined, and governments are deprived of the revenue to maintain necessary public services. Similarly, international competition leads firms to press governments to delay implementing stricter controls to combat climate change and local pollution. Both physical and social sustainability are thus threatened.

8. **Economic globalization and social exclusion.** As a result of market integration millions of jobs are lost at the level of production, meaning that more and more people are affected by chronic unemployment, lack the necessary means for a decent life and confront the painful realization that their socio-economic rights are of little or no importance. The mergers and take-overs which are a chief index of globalization are often followed by an announcement that jobs are being cut. At the level of international trade, certain regions of the world, such as Africa and Central America, have a smaller share today than twenty years ago. This greatly affects the life of many people, whose only chance for survival is the informal sector, "the underground economy", where their social rights are not respected.

9. **Motorized mobility and increasing migration.** Mobility has always been a driving force of trade; and the present level of world trade would not be possible

without the development of more and faster transportation of both persons and goods. Further expanding world trade favours the further increase of motorized mobility. From the point of view of sustainability, this must be avoided. Those concerned with the environmental crisis believe that new approaches to mobility and transport must be found.

A further element of mobility is reflected in the increasing numbers of uprooted people. The phenomenon of economic refugees has reached an intensity unforeseen as recently as ten years ago. When the conditions to survive decently are lacking in their native places, people decide to migrate - from rural areas to the cities, from small towns to the big urban centres, from poor countries to wealthier ones. However, prevailing economic trends are unable to create the conditions necessary to enable societies to face this situation adequately. Indeed, the integration of markets is managed a way that works against this. The result is a growth of lawlessness and violence both in the North and the South. Current demographic trends, especially in the South, tend to aggravate this.

10. **Intercultural tensions.** When economic globalization is affirmed as the only route to a better human future, those cultures which experience its impact as a threat or even an attack will inevitably clash with prevailing trends. Cultural fragmentation is almost inescapable. People's lives are torn. They cannot reject integration into international markets and the accompanying imperatives to be more efficient and competitive; at the same time, they sense that their traditions, values and identities (which often include a respectful and caring attitude to the natural environment) are in danger. These tensions are sometimes unfortunately manifested in violent terms.

11. **The role of the state.** A key structural consequence of globalization has been a weakening of political control over economic life. In an earlier era, the shift of power from the local to the national level, which was a characteristic element in the formation of the modern nation-state, disrupted local community but provided the ground for a less parochial assessment of the social conditions necessary for human life. But the contemporary reduction of national political power and sovereignty has not been compensated for by the creation of a transnational political authority which could appropriately and democratically define the limits within which market activity must occur. International economic and especially financial exchanges strive to limit the control of national authorities.

In this context, the regulatory role of the state in the economic realm must be underlined. If the state should not be an economic actor among others, competing with them, it ought nevertheless to set the framework and to be responsible for the economic process at the national level, including its economic exchanges with other nations. Both Christian ethics and good secular policy analysis require a careful coordination of these processes. It is irresponsible for the wealthiest groups of the world to press for quick international agreements that so evidently serve their own interests while postponing and resisting morally necessary agreements in areas such as labour standards and environmental policies because they would place limits on the freedom of firms and the consumption of the prosperous. It is the responsibility of the state to guarantee that the common national interest is respected; and to do so it must fulfil its regulatory role.

COMMUNITIES IN A CONTEXT OF GLOBALIZATION

Human beings seek meaning and the experience of belonging to associations with other persons with whom they can develop face-to-face and not only "virtual" relationships. Such contacts are far easier in places where tradition prevails and people know each other on a personal level than in societies more strongly affected by modernity.

It is important to recognize the role that different types of human communities play. Though not all persons participate in community life, those who do participate experience a strengthening of their personal identity. This kind of human relationship is more meaningful than that which characterizes life in mass society. In community life people share common concerns, mutual support and solidarity. To be sure, human communities are never perfect, but they do create a space where dialogue is possible and where life can be more human.

Some communities share interests which enable their members to involve themselves in some common action. Through this they express common convictions and common responsibilities. The community then becomes something more than a mere human association. It is like an organism, which expresses itself as a collective being in particular tones about matters which are of common concern. Thus communities can be clearly distinguished within mass society. Though their members may be involved in all kinds of social processes, they are particularly known by how they relate to other members of their community and by the kind of common thought and action that they develop.

All human societies, in one way or another, are influenced by the different elements involved in the process of globalization. The impact of new technologies of communications and the integration of markets have a direct or indirect impact on people's lives. The social relationships which globalization favours are those which are "virtual" and less personal. That is, the prevailing trends of the global economy privilege that which is more characteristic of the life of mass society - mass communications, mass consumption, homogenization of patterns of life, mass culture. (Again, however, we must be reminded that globalization is a complex process, and both comprehensive endorsement or blanket rejection of it is morally and conceptually simplistic.)

In the context of mass society, human beings run the risk of being depersonalized. A tension emerges between society and communities, especially those communities which support causes and concerns that are not well respected in social life, whether in the economic, political, cultural or even religious realm. This happens, for example, to communities which affirm and defend the sustainability of nature and of human societies. At the level of the village or the nation or the region or the planet, they try to initiate social processes which can make life more human, more personal. To put it another way, they try to introduce a dose of what they believe is *good sense* in the *common sense* which prevails among the majority of the people.

These communities cannot avoid tension and confrontation with prevailing trends of economic globalization. And if they are not aware of their vulnerability and limitations, they risk losing their identity. But at the same time, they can strengthen themselves if they are also aware of their *charisma*, of the authority that they can play in society so long as they are faithful to their vocation. If power in mass society is linked to numbers of people, the authority of communities can be based only on their quality. They can make an impact, even if their action is not comparable with the magnitude of the powers which give direction to life in mass society. This impact depends on the inherent character of the community, its courage to be and to support its convictions. It is a matter of ethical decision.

PRESENT GLOBAL TRENDS AND COMMUNITY LIFE

Some elements of the process of globalization as we have described it open up possibilities for community life. Technological developments accelerate and multiply at least virtual communications. Information is disseminated more widely; international networks are built up. Accompanying these opportunities is the emergence of an international civil society as the expression of the will of many civil (non-governmental) people's associations, which affirm public interests such as respect for the environment, justice for the needy and human rights. In some way or another, people's movements also benefit from some facets of globalization.

However, globalization also threatens community life. First, given its dependence on the world of human constructions and the extraordinary nature of most of the elements which make it possible, globalization accentuates the instrumental intention of economic activities. It reinforces a "culture of enterprise" which reduces most created beings to things and means. Human beings, who can understand themselves only by taking account of their living relationships with their environment, run the risk of having an important part of themselves amputated. The breaking of communion between nature and human beings tempts persons to ignore not only their links with their environment but also their own limits. The sacramental dimension of life, its mystery, is no longer recognized.

Unfortunately, experiences show that instrumentality seldom takes account of the unintended consequences of instrumental action. One of these is precisely its effect on the character of human communities. Reduced to tools in social processes, they risk losing their potential to be spaces in which human beings can create meaning for their lives.

A second threat comes from the peculiar ideological proposal - *la pensée unique* - which accompanies the process of globalization and aspires to be the only valid one, imposing itself as the paradigm to which all other cultures should be adjusted. Human communities come to be and live in their own specific cultural contexts. The difference among these contexts should be respected. The homogenization of human behaviour which global markets implicitly intend to impose endangers community life by threatening people's relationships with their own cultures and by depersonalizing human relationships.

Third, when many human beings use only virtual communications to relate to each other, adopting a dominant code of signs as common language, and therefore neglecting other languages, the result is a loss in the quality of being of a community. Virtual relationships depersonalize human contacts. Mass culture, conveyed by an increasing use of mass media, continues to expand. It also results in mass consumption. The danger of cultural fragmentation is almost unavoidable.

Fourth, the particularly devastating effects of the prevailing trends of the globalizing economy on the community life of indigenous peoples must be particularly emphasized. Exploitation of natural resources and lack of care for land often threaten the very being of these communities.

COMMUNITIES AND CARING FOR LIFE

Those who want to manage the processes and integration of markets favour globalization. They look on its development optimistically, encouraged by the unprecedented growth in world trade. They believe the integration of markets will bring along with it the integration of cultures and peoples.

However, many others are fearful and anxious about the high price they must pay to adjust themselves to globalization. Still others simply feel lost. Those who are excluded from the process of globalization experience pain, suffering and meaninglessness. They feel that they are not recognized but are considered as objects, as masses, but not as human beings with rights and responsibilities. As part of the mass of excluded people - whether they live in industrialized, developing or less developed nations - they sense that they are despised and discarded, as if they do not count at all. They do not have the chance to live well, but only to survive. The underground economy seems to be their only chance.

Amidst this paradoxical coexistence of the integration of markets and the exclusion of people are some communities in which men and women associate to affirm life. Not surprisingly, many of the individuals who participate in groups defending human rights are also involved in the ecological movement and in other movements acting for social renewal. The common thread is their affirmation of life - an expression of their awareness that we share a common existence in a world where injustice prevails and life is in danger. These communities ask whether sustainability has a chance within the context of ongoing globalization. Can a sustainable society emerge in the framework of prevailing trends of growing world trade and human mobility? Is it possible to launch processes of "sustainable development"?

Such communities are ready to resist the threats globalization poses to human beings and to sustain and affirm a kind of life which is common to all and can be shared with future generations. These communities, which care for life and intend to resist irresponsible behaviour, are aware not only of their limited possibilities but also of their convictions and of their responsibilities.

These are *ethical communities*. They practise ethical discernment, on the basis of which they perceive both what must be affirmed and what is unacceptable. In order to affirm their convictions they undertake actions for sustainability. Confronted with what should not be accepted, they involve themselves in resistance. Both - affirmation and resistance - are two sides of the same coin: *caring for life*. These communities show themselves to be aware that the fundamental solidarity among all human beings, and above all with the poor and oppressed, cannot and should not be dissolved, that the mystery of the communion between human beings and the natural environment must be acknowledged and respected, that life is more than *my* life and so I cannot treat life as an object.

Ethical communities, aware of their convictions and responsibilities, have values for which they are ready to pay the price. Values remain in the realm of the subjective up to the moment when those who affirm them are prepared to substantiate that affirmation with a costly action. Sometimes this means resisting ideas and social behaviours which are shared by the majority of the people, resisting the prevailing *common sense*, because it is not *good sense*. The uncritical affirmation and absolutization of the globalization process is not *good sense*, no matter how large the masses who see it as the only way into the future. Rather than accepting and supporting an instrumental approach to reality, *good sense* expresses the conviction that the mystery (sacrament) of life is to be cared for, and that responsible action must follow this awareness.

CHRISTIAN CHURCHES AS COMMUNITIES OF MEANING AND GRACE

Many Christians are involved in different types of communities which are concerned for the sustainability of life. There are Christian communities that witness to their faith by striving for justice and solidarity and caring for the environment. These communities try to understand the situations in which they live and to analyze their different aspects. They also study the Bible for inspiration and guidance for action. And when they decide to get involved in praxis, they do it collectively, as a fellowship. As they share the means of grace, they also share their commitment.

This awareness of faith overcomes the separation between culture and nature, between history and creation. The love commandment involves God and the human neighbour (individuals, social groups, future generations), but also the rest of creation. Because the mystery of God's grace has no limits, Christian communities witness to this grace and seek to introduce the awareness of this faith into a world whose powers do not want to recognize it.

Christian communities face the challenge of translating their awareness of faith to society, of making more clear the meaning of grace through social structures and institutions. They know that their witness is often only a very limited and symbolic testimony to the presence of grace in what seems a graceless world. Thus they try to be the "salt of the earth" and "the light of the world". A praxis of sustainability and action aimed at shaping a sustainable society, caring for justice, the environment and solidarity, are necessary components of Christian witness in our time.

When globalization is affirmed as the only way, it becomes sacralized. An idol is shaped, a fetish is crafted. A false god justifies the striving for domination of powerful agents who respect neither nature nor their neighbours' rights. Christians are called to confess that God is gracious and just, and that God cannot be confused with Mammon.

THEOLOGICAL INSIGHTS:

THE DOUBLE CHALLENGE OF SUSTAINABILITY AND JUSTICE

One of the convictions of faith that provides meaning for Christians is an awareness of the sacramental dimension of all creation. The creation speaks about the Creator (Pss. 19:1-6; 104:1-30). This is not "natural revelation", but an awareness that in mysterious ways the imprint of God and his eternal love and plan are present in creation. Creation is not finished, and Christian communities expect and hope for the fulfilment of God's work, in which they have been graciously invited to collaborate (cf. 2 Cor. 5:16-6:2).

For Christian communities, care for the creation is thus unavoidable. This demands a concerted action of caring for one's neighbour and caring for the social and the natural environment.

Christian faithfulness requires living in a right relationship with the whole of the created world. This means living within the natural limits of the created world, treating it as an integral part of God's creation, and tending to nature in order to increase and to use its bounty without destroying it, so that it may provide for successive generations.

Christian faithfulness also requires living in a right relationship with the rest of humanity, which is also a part of creation. This means recognizing one's obligation to treat the other as an integral part of God's creation, to care for the other as an end in himself or herself, not a mere means to an end. Thus Christians regard both the natural world and the human social world which it shelters as having intrinsic worth and as being intricately connected. They are worthy and of value in and of themselves, as part of creation, just because they are.

Christians remember that Jesus made love of the neighbour one of the core ethical injunctions of the Christian faith. As we consider the processes of globalization, we must admit that these economic processes not only exploit and ruin nature, far exceeding its natural limits and regenerative abilities, but also exploit human beings, condemning many millions of urban and rural workers to generations of poverty, and altogether excluding many millions more from formal economic and political life. Such exploitation and exclusionism is wrong. It is a clear violation of the intrinsic worth of both the human person and the natural world. As Christians we must insist on and work for acceptable alternatives. Not to do so is tantamount to the literal sacrifice of perhaps billions of human beings in successive generations on the altar of market processes and market ideology, human expediency and greed.

THE TEMPTATION OF IDOLATRY

The complacency of the comfortable can easily become a form of idolatry. Without thinking about it, they passively allow the market to assume the properties and dimensions of God in their imaginations and in their behaviour. People come to accept the fate meted out by the market as if submission were the only option. Thus what is in actuality a mere mechanism devised by human beings to foster efficient production and consumption takes on the proportions of an autonomous force governing the lives of individuals and communities.

Again and again the Bible warns against this tendency to create institutions and practices which come over time to be seen as autonomous and independent of their creators, this inclination to submit to their logic, accept them as inevitable and thus worship limited human creations instead of the creator God. Consider, for example, the Golden Calf in Exodus 32, shaped out of the melted gold of many people and then worshipped as God. The biblical name for this behaviour is idolatry, and it is understood as a primary source of human sin.

The biblical writers insisted that we cannot worship God while worshipping our own human creations as if they were God. We cannot serve our neighbour when sacrificing him or her to the false gods we have created and upon which we in our insecurity have come to depend.

The biblical texts remind us that we are not the first to create and to worship false gods. But the magnitude and scope of the processes of the global market seem to make it clear that in no previous idolatry has so much been at stake, both in terms of the survival of many millions of human beings and in terms of the planet earth itself.

One cannot expect to dismantle this idolatry of the global market economy without unmasking this idol, making clear the relationships, bringing to visibility much of what is today hidden and mysterious. Christians must confess and denounce these relationships and then begin the process of reconstruction. Rich and poor, in North and South, must confess their idolatrous relationship with the global market economy in different ways. Some will have to confess to participating in the construction of that economy, others to perpetuating its ideology. Some will have to confess the easy compliance of the comfortable, others their willingness to sacrifice all values and traditions to the illusory promise of the market's glitter.

Too many Christians, especially the rich, have identified Christianity with market economics, attributing to the market Christian virtues and values, and importing market values and practices into their understanding of the Christian faith. In some quarters a critique of the global market is perceived as an attack on Christianity itself. Many have identified material success with spiritual well-being, implicitly and sometimes explicitly concluding that poverty is the proof of the material and spiritual failure of the poor. But the poor know better than the rich that material wealth is no sign of spiritual wealth. From the depths of their own experience they understand Jesus' repeated warning that wealth is more often than not a hindrance rather than a help to faithful clarity of vision and purpose.

The Christian God is not the global market, nor does God require the sacrifice of humans and nature to market processes. Faithfulness today requires not total submission to the lure and the power of global market processes, but rather participation in the creation and re-creation of human institutions and practices which support values of inclusion rather than exclusion, protection rather than destruction, stewardship rather than greed, solidarity rather than the survival of the fittest.

A PLEA FOR CRITICAL REALISM

Just as Christians must not succumb to the temptation of idolatry, so they should not be misled by romantic and idealistic visions of a perfect state of things. There is no perfect society. Though obliged to unmask and resist the idolatry inherent in the present system, Christians should not suppose or suggest that there will ever be a society guaranteeing justice, peace and full harmony with creation. Guided by the values of the gospel message, they will seek to participate in setting up structures that promote the widest possible participation. They will seek to strengthen respect for the dignity of all, especially the vulnerable and weak. They will give priority to the demands of solidarity. But they are conscious that human life is replete with competing forces and that the order and functioning of society are inevitably based on compromises. Within the complex network of modern society, the best possible solutions must be responsibly pursued.

The institutions and initiatives which sustain the values of justice, peace and respect for the environment will be multiple and varied. Christians will regard them as limited human instruments, the product of human communities all over the globe, the result of life lived together, thus containing conflicting understandings and interests and established in a form that will change over time. Making room for such institutions requires social, political and economic analysis; and initiatives for evaluation can be thwarted by the absence of a critical overall assessment of the state of society. But the primary concern will be with building up communities that witness to the love of both the neighbour and the whole created world. Some of these communities may not be explicitly Christian. But Christians will not hesitate to work with any group or movement responding to the twofold call to sustainability and justice.

NOTES

[1] Michael Kinnamon, ed., *Signs of the Spirit*, report of the WCC's seventh assembly, Geneva, WCC, 1991, p.78; cf. the "Statement on Issues Arising out of Developments in Central and Eastern Europe", *Minutes of the 41st Meeting of the WCC Central Committee, March 1990*, Geneva, WCC, 1990, pp.50-53.

[2] *Christian Faith and the World Economy Today*, Geneva, WCC, 1992, p.17.

[3] David M. Paton, ed., *Breaking Barriers: Nairobi 1975*, Geneva, WCC, 1976, p.127.

[4] *Study Encounter 69*, vol. 10, no.4, 1974, p.2.

[5] *Sustainable Growth: A Contradiction in Terms*, Geneva, Visser 't Hooft Endowment Fund for Ecumenical Leadership, 1993, p.5.

Appendix IIIc.

Batista, Israel, "Social Movements: A Personal Testimony", *Social Movements,* *Globalization, Exclusion* **(Geneva: WCC, 1997), pp. 1-7.**

This paper does not aim to provide a "synthesis" of the richness contained in this dossier on "Social Movements: Challenges and Dilemmas". This task belongs to all and each one of us. I believe this is not yet a time for final synthesis. We need to provide more spaces for conversations, common actions and even discussions. Sometimes some of our syntheses have led us into imposed models of unity. We are on the way to build alliances, solidarity, self-esteem and dignity. Let us continue this way.

The purpose of my paper is very simple:

First,   a call for discernment. – The readiness to foster our imagination in the searching for new signs and visions.

Second,   a wish for dreams. – The ability to wish, to dream is part of being human. The activities of social movements in society reveal the patience and endurance of ordinary women and men, their capacity to resist and even to dream in the midst of injustices.

Third,   a personal witness. – To share my experiences of my contacts with social movements in many corners of the globe. I hope to make a humble contribution in order to energize utopias, to strengthen people's aspirations for the building of sustainable societies, and to encourage imaginations and creativity in the search for alternatives and paradigms.

I.- Could utopia become reality?

We are accustomed to interpreting history assuming that certain trends are unchanged, or internalizing some factors in a way that paralyses our creativity. A number of well-known and well founded realities are quoted as if they were a "rosary of calamities" with no solution: concentration of power, brokenness of models, exclusion of majorities, mass culture imposition, increased impoverishment, etc. In spite of these crude facts, reality is more unforeseen….., praise the Lord! Life is more dynamic….., this is our hope.

Sometimes we are forerunners of calamity, but we are not always ready to read the signs of the time from people's daily experiences in the midst of history. Let me insist that when comprehensive alternatives are not in place, even in view, it is most important to look for evidence, for starting points of resistance and to encourage new visions and perspectives.

Within this unpredictable historical situation we find two main approaches in the search for responses:

1. Defensive structural attitudes: Institutional structures – political, economic, social and religious ones - have tended to adopt defensive and less cooperative and ecumenical positions in the attempt to preserve the institutional life of their organization.

2. People's cooperation and solidarity: We also find, not without tensions, an ecumenical concern in the question for alternative ways of living in the social life of grassroots groups and organizations that are struggling for specific goals. People feel the need to meet and look together for common solutions. We need one another at this time when no one holds the monopoly of truth. A spirit of cooperation and solidarity is slowly growing out of practical social actions.

I would like to share some criteria that could be important to have in mind when addressing the issue of utopia and alternatives:

1. Plurality and diversity are more important than homogeneity. The way of unity comes through the diversities of our own identities.

2. While not neglecting the importance of plurality, a major trend today in people's movements is the search for inter-actions across diversities, solidarity across specificities, and the coming together with others to build alliances of hope.

3. The world needs new visions of global cooperation for the next century. Global analysis and global vision complement, rather than substitute specific national struggles. Social action, advocacy, activities and solidarity are an inter-marriage of both global and local realities, action and reflection processes.

4.   People's empowerment is concerned with the human realities in all activities. From production to institutional changes, from political struggle to human needs.

5.   Social action and cooperation have to do with conviction and commitment. The lack of personal and community involvement is often the real cause of our failures. Political and social alliances and commitments are an option, not a chance.

6.   The need to move our spirits from polarization to the rediscovering of the potentials of unity and common actions. The need to accompany our resistance with a spirit of reconstruction and of pro-active responses.

In the World Council of Churches (WCC), we are using the idea of Jubilee in the Bible as a vision open to the future. "The proclamation of Jubilee is not a prolongation of what is known, it includes risks, but also gives birth to new hopes", as one of the WCC papers states. Not moved by a proselytising interest, allow me to use the richness of this concept according to our understandings.

■   <u>Jubilee as a gift of God</u> – Jubilee has to do with the promises of God in history. It is the affirmation of our confidence in God's grace. The proclamation of God's daily grace for the excluded people in moments of fragility.

■   <u>The pilgrim character of Jubilee</u> – Jubilee is not simply the search for justice. It is an attempt to provide a comprehensive and symbolic vision during transitional periods, in which justice is an essential element. The Jubilee means a kind of new beginning, a general overhaul of economic, cultural and social life in order to restore persons, creation and property to their rightful condition, a door to the future.

■   <u>The Jubilee is celebration</u> – The Jubilee is an imaginative alternative to the prevailing criteria of exclusion. It is the feast of the Spirit that celebrates life-centered valued in the midst of despair.

■   <u>The Jubilee as a "conspiracy" against the routine of the charisma.</u> – It has a constructive character rather than an analytical capacity. We are used to "business as usual", the routine of well-known behaviour patterns. The proclamation of Jubilee moves us to a radical conversion: The inertia has gone and imagination precedes our actions and activities.

II. – <u>Globalization and imagination.</u>

Whether globalization is a myth or reality, it is a process that cannot be ignored because of its implications for the life of the people in their communities. This is a world of hegemonic imposition available only for "chosen persons", a world in which a model of exclusion is imposed. These are facts.

Therefore, this is a moment when thoughtful analysis, appropriate questions and challenging actions are required. The present globalization of the world could respond to what Robert Heilbroner, in "The Future as History", calls "the fresh sense of what to do". A kind of Western activism that has been used by the financial and economic forces to bring the world to the situation they wanted. We are impatient to act, but let us avoid certain pragmatism which looks for "fast food" solutions. We have to learn how to live without any alternatives in place and without envisaging any in the short term. We have to learn to be like gardeners sowing and cultivating the many different flowers that may spring up.

I am not neglecting the devastating consequences of the present financial and economic globalization. As examples, we can point to some features of this reality:

- The Uruguayan writer Eduardo Galeano explains: "Never has the world been so unequal in terms of opportunities it provides, nor so equalizing in terms of ideas and customs".

- In the 60's the theory of dependence made room for a certain space for independence. Now this theory is obsolete: we are expressing total submission, total dependence. Even more, some countries are dispensable for the world market.

- The pragmatic analysis of economists and financiers is based on the principle of exclusion. Growing poverty and exclusion have become a dominant social political development of our era. Inequality and exclusion are not distortions of the system. They are a systemic requisite for growth and permanence.

- Supranationalism contributes to the nation-state's loss of influence over its own economic affairs. Robert Heilbroner again says: "the problems of international trade and finances.....bring many the uneasy suspicion that the basic unity of economic policy, the nation- state, is not appropriate to the problems of the late twentieth century capitalism".

■ Robert D. Kaplan believes that the twenty-first century will see radical environmental degradation and tribal violence in an effort by communities and cultures to survive an increasingly anarchic situation.

These tensions and dilemmas do not justify a return to merely ideological confrontations. This is a time for imagination and creativity. These realities call upon us for new visions and perspectives. We have reached a point in history where prophetic denunciations are useless if they are not accompanied by suggested alternatives. That makes it all the more important to look for starting points of resistance and to encourage new visions and perspectives.

It is crucial to address a number of dramatic realities that are influencing people's activities in society. A few key points include:

■ The "triumphalism" of the world market system does not mean that justice reigns. However, how to resist dramatic facts which promote criteria that perpetuate injustice?

— The subliminal message suggesting that outside the existing economic system there is no salvation.

— The acceptance of social costs and human sufferings as inevitable and necessary.

— The imposition of adjustment economic policies as unavoidable decisions.

■ "Accountability" and "legitimacy" are key words in assessing the exercise of power in society. These values must apply in all kinds of relationships in society, i.e., from the institutions that dominate the international financial and economic system to the affirmation of human rights in every context. In this sense, contradictions are perceived between democracy and economy. Democracy as the right to life for all is incompatible with the present economic policies. What has been called "common sense" is not necessarily "good sense" for people's lives.

- We may say that alternatives or paradigms are more related to local contexts. Nevertheless, the logic of the dominant financial and economic system is rather different; concentration of power at a global level, transnationalization of the economy, a single world order, a global village and a homogeneous mass culture in order to impose conditions at the local level.

How do we approach global and local realities within the present globalization process in which fragmentation is also a reality?

- The new symbiosis among science, technology, production and sales both strengthens and intensifies major structural changes in international markets. A new transnational division of production is in its own way, not based on assigning value to natural resource, but mainly on an internal division of knowledge and installed human capacity.

- Ethical values for political decisions and the setting of priorities in situations of survival are sometimes in opposition with the pragmatic management solutions proposed for resolving the crisis. Two outstanding principles are at stake:

  a. The principle of a life-centred economy rooted in justice and love is being confronted with the pragmatic principles of the world economy: efficiency, success, profit, growth, competence and privatization.
  b. The traditional understanding of the "basic needs" calls for a broader approach that includes human aspirations, subjective factors and the dimension of life in creation.

I do not want to be captive of old ideological schemes. Matyas Rakosi, a former Hungarian Communist Party leader, asked on one occasion: "Comrades, have we sunk so low as to be taken in by our own propaganda?" I do not want to be caught up in "slogans" and "ideological schemes" which do not represent people's aspirations. My concern is to avoid "running business as usual", or in the name of "post-modernism" to be trapped in the rationale of the hegemonic system.

I believe in the importance of making a distinction between this hegemonic market global system, that we cannot ignore or escape, and the aspiration for a "universal community across diversities" or, the promotion of an "international solidarity" or, as a "transborder alliance of hope." Let us commit the best of ourselves in these two directions:

a. Let us open spaces within this hegemonic globalization. Let us use all our imagination, patience and endurance to expand people's possibilities and to promote solidarity and cooperation across borders and diversities.

b. Let us join efforts to promote a "new international civil society" in which the following could be possible:

1. The development of new values serving the needs of the people and respecting human/people rights.

2. The search for more participatory forms of democracy and participation.

3. The strengthening of ordinary people's capacity of taking responsibilities for decisions, actions and conditions in everyday life.

4. The establishment of new international mechanisms of governance.

III. What is the meaning of hope in our world scenario?

People seen socially are not identical to people seen politically. We cannot ignore the attempts and even the success in the strategy of the neo-liberal system in controlling and manipulating people's aspirations. Approaching people's struggles means to be aware of hope and frustrations, faith and despair, resistance and manipulation.

What kind of challenges do I perceive in the world arena that could be relevant for our concern on social movements? Many indications can be found in the different papers of this dossier. I do not pretend to exhaust the list of possibilities. I would simply want to address four major considerations for social movements in society affirming the diversities according to the different contexts.

1. A culture of solidarity in society. – One of the most important challenges which we face lies in the strengthening and organization of social spaces. Strategies of taking over power, very prominent in the past, are rarely feasible today. The question is to build power from below keeping in mind processes and long-term strategies. Without slipping into an overly triumphant attitude, it is necessary to strengthen civil society's role as an expression of anti-systemic resistance. We are not for pure activism. The issue at stake is the capacity of social movements' organizations to ask for accountability to the state and the economy.

Social and political organizations are taking place in the space of civil society. They are new emerging powers born of the heat of resistance and survival. They are embryonic forms of doing politics. The bases of these movements can be found in the social solidarity in daily life, in social resistance to disintegration, in cultural affirmation in the face of homogenization, in denouncement and mobilisation on the part of new social actors and a result of different rationality in setting priorities. Important tasks are envisaged at the level of civil society:

■ Create new paradigms and alternatives for social expression which are connected to culture, spirituality and to connect the realities of daily life with social, political and economic systems.

■ Strengthen the accountability capacity of people and social movements' organizations.

A new culture of solidarity is emerging in society linked to the survival of the people in daily life and to the matter of resistance in relation with cultural identity. A new ecumenical spirit of cooperation and solidarity is developing among the people. Partnerships in the search for new paradigms and common action on concrete concerns inspire these encounters. While single issues and specific identities are important, people are looking for more inter-relations and new social configurations.

A process of redefinition of different social actors is making our societies more dynamic. Even old actors are redefining their role in different ways, for example trade unions. These social actors take their place in society according to their need, to their subjectivity and identities, and not necessarily on the basis of ideology and politics.

2. <u>A culture of life.</u> – The current world situation confronts us with new realities in relation to life and the survival of the people. In many places people have identified the issue of life as the vital concern in the struggles.

■ Any alternative form of economic life that does not take into consideration the cultural and religious values of the people is invalid.

■ Economic activity has to guarantee life in all its dimensions: human needs and aspirations, regeneration of the natural cycle and the protection of the basis of life for future generations.

3.	*Globalization and national infrastructures.* – Since there is no counter-acting power to pressure international organizations for implementation of global issues, since the end of the Cold War has brought arrogance and hegemonic patterns at a global level, there is the feeling of help-lessness due to the fact that we are at the mercy of international financial organizations. This is why global analysis and global linkages are urgently needed. What does it mean today to make the world powers accountable to the people?

The diminishing role of the state makes the financial powers less and less accountable. There is an increased concern among social groups to do research on the need for a more solid and different kind of state. There is a priority to discuss the role of the nation-state in a frame of globalization.

Parallel to such developments, we are experiencing at national and local levels, how groups are getting in touch with each other and form-ing networks of action. The question is how to strengthen the infrastruc-tural capacities of these entities at a national level. The emergence of social movements demands the building of solid people-oriented organ-izations, strong infrastructures and relevant means of communication.

4.	Human promotion. – We need to invest in people. Human promotion is concerned with developing human capacities which allow people to participate in social, political and economic decisions and to work cre-atively toward the future. Human promotion includes knowledge and technology, management and skills, training and education, participa-tion and organization.

Participation should not be confused with "activism", reflection should not be disqualified as "intellectualism", training should not be under-stood as "manipulation". In the midst of many challenges, processes of reflection, analysis, training and organization are important in order to expand people's empowerment. Searching for paradigms demands critical thinking and clear visions. We need to move beyond the old conflict between action and reflection, praxis and analysis. We need to reconcile mind, heart and body.

The capacities to dream, to wish, to resist in hope are all part of people's struggles. Let us allow hope to bloom. Hope is essential in people's resistance. At the same time, let us deepen our capacity of discernment of dreams and utopias. However, today it is not enough to dream or to promote utopias. Today we are challenged to make utopias a reality in the midst of history, to make these utopias come true.

Appendix IIId.

"Ten Affirmations on Justice, Peace and the Integrity of Creation," *Now is the Time: The Final Document and Other Texts from the World Convocation on Justice, Peace and the Integrity of Creation*, Geneva: WCC, 1990, pp. 11-21.

Introduction

In this world marked by injustice, violence and degradation of the environment we want to reaffirm God's covenant which is open to all and holds the promise of life in wholeness and right relationships. Responding to God's covenant we profess our faith in the Triune God who is the very source of communion.

Our response to the covenant today leads us to make the following affirmations on urgent issues where justice, peace and the integrity of creation are at stake. They represent firm convictions that have grown out of years of ecumenical dialogue and struggle.

We make these affirmations as Christian people aware that many people of living faiths and ideologies share these concerns with us and are guided by their understanding of justice, peace and the integrity of creation. We therefore seek dialogue and cooperation with them, guided by a vision of the new future which is necessary for the survival for our planet.

We can only make these affirmations as we acknowledge our shortcomings and failures and commit ourselves anew to the reality of God's reign. This means to resist in thought, word and action the powers of separation and destruction and to live in active solidarity with the suffering people.

AFFIRMATION I

We affirm that all exercise of power is accountable to God

The world belongs to God. Therefore, all forms of human power and exercise of authority should serve God's purposes in the world and are answerable to the people on whose behalf they are exercised. Those who wield power - economic, political, military, social, scientific, cultural, legal, religious - must be stewards of

God's justice and peace. In Christ, God's power is demonstrated in redemptive suffering, as compassionate love which identifies itself with broken and suffering humanity. This empowers people to proclaim the message of liberation, love and hope which offers new life, to resist injustice and to struggle against the powers of death.

Therefore we affirm that all forms of human power and authority are subject to God and accountable to people. This means the right of people to full participation. In Christ, God decisively revealed the meaning of power as compassionate love that prevails over the forces of death.

We will resist any exercise of power and authority which tries to monopolize power and so prohibits processes of transformation towards justice, peace and integrity of creation.

We commit ourselves to support the constructive power of people's movements in their struggle for human dignity and liberation as well as in achieving just and participatory forms of government and economic structures.

AFFIRMATION II

We affirm God's option for the poor

The poor are the exploited and oppressed. Their poverty is not accidental. It is very often a result of deliberate policies which result in the constantly increasing accumulation of wealth and power in the hands of a few. The existence of poverty is a scandal and a crime. It is blasphemy to say that it is the will of God. Jesus came that we should have "life in all its fullness" (John 10:10). In his death and resurrection, Christ exposed and thereby conquered the powers that deny the poor their right to abundant life (Luke 4:16-21). God shows a preferential option for the poor. "The glory of God is reflected in the poor person fully alive" (Archbishop Romero). In the cries of the poor we hear the challenging voice of God.

Those whom society treats as "the least" are described by Jesus as his sisters and brothers (Matthew 25:31-46). While we support the need for diaconal services and urgent response to emergencies, we recognize in our time that the needs of "the least" can only be met by fundamentally transforming the world economy through structural change. Charity and aid projects alone cannot meet the needs and protect the dignity of the world's poorest billion people of whom women and children are the majority. The solution to the debt crisis can only be found through a just, equitable world economic order and not in palliative measures like the re-scheduling of debts.

We <u>affirm</u> God's preferential option for the poor and state that as Christians our duty is to embrace God's action in the struggles of the poor in the liberation of us all.

We <u>will resist </u>all forces, policies and institutions which create and perpetuate poverty or accept it as inevitable and ineradicable.

We <u>commit</u> ourselves to be allies of those organizations and efforts which are dedicated to achieving the eradication of exploitation and oppression.

AFFIRMATION III

We affirm the equal value of all races and peoples

In Jesus Christ, all people of whatever race, caste, or ethnic descent are reconciled to God and to each other. Racism as an ideology and discrimination as a practice are renunciations of the rich diversity of God's design for the world and violations of the dignity of human personality. All forms of racism - whether individual, collective or systemic - must be named sin and their theological justification heresy.

We reject the perversion of the language of human and peoples' rights to assert so-called "group rights", an assertion which is divisive and seeks not to liberate but to preserve economic exploitation and political privilege by powerful minorities.

Therefore, remembering the covenant of God who declares "All the families of the earth are mine":

We <u>affirm</u> that people of every race, caste and ethnic group are of equal value. In the very diversity of their cultures and traditions, they reflect the rich plurality of God's creation.

We <u>will resist</u> the denial of the rights of human beings who are members of exploited and oppressed racial, ethnic, caste or indigenous groups. We will resist attempts by dominant cultures and groups to deprive them of their cultural identity, full citizenship and equal access to economic, social, political and ecclesial power. We will resist the oppression and exploitation of women and children belonging to these oppressed groups. They are the ones who are the most painfully affected.

We therefore <u>commit</u> ourselves to work against the forces of racism, ethnicism and casteism and to stand in solidarity with their victims and their struggles.

AFFIRMATION IV

We affirm that male and female are created in the image of God

In God's image God created male and female (Genesis 1:27). This creation in God's image is the basis for a dynamic relationship between women and men for the transformation of society. Christ affirmed the personhood of women and empowered them to a life of dignity and fullness. Women with men, as "new creation in Christ" (2 Corinthians 5:17) must work towards a world where all forms of discrimination are eliminated. Therefore, as we remember the covenant of God:

We <u>affirm</u> the creative power given to women to stand for life wherever there is death. In Jesus' community women find acceptance and dignity and with them he shared the imperative to carry the good news.

We <u>will resist</u> structures of patriarchy which perpetuate violence against women in their homes and in a society which has exploited their labour and sexuality. Within this we pay special attention to the most vulnerable women - those who are poor and/or black, Dalits, members of indigenous communities, refugees, migrant workers and women of other oppressed groups. We will resist all structures of dominance which exclude the theological and spiritual contributions of women and deny their participation in decision-making processes in church and society.

Therefore, encouraged by the persistence of women in their struggles for life, all over the world, we <u>commit</u> ourselves to seek ways of realizing a new community of women and men.

AFFIRMATION V

We affirm that truth is at the foundation of a community of free people

Jesus Christ lived a life of truthfulness. In living God's truth he got into conflict with the values and powers of his society. He communicated his message of truth to the people, teaching and preaching with simple language, images and examples.

People's abilities to communicate and learn are among the greatest gifts of God. They relate and bind individuals together into communities, and communities into the one human family. Communication and education in the service of justice, peace and the integrity of creation carry an awe-inspiring responsibility for the future.

The prophet Zechariah says, "These are things you should do: Speak the truth to one another. In the courts give real justice - the kind that makes for peace" (Zechariah 8:16).

Today, new technologies offer possibilities of wider communication and education for all. At the same time their misuse threatens the true purpose of communication and education. Ignorance, illiteracy, propaganda, misinformation and sheer falsehood face us; therefore, as we respond to the God of the truth that sets us free:

> We <u>affirm</u> that access to truth and education, information and means of communication are basic human rights. All people have the right to be educated, to tell their own stories, to speak their own convictions and beliefs, to be heard by others and to have the power to distinguish truth from falsehood.

> We <u>will resist</u> policies that deny freedom of expression; that encourage the concentration of the communication media in the hands of the state or of economically powerful monopolies; that tolerate the spread of consumerism,

racism, casteism, sexism, chauvinism in all its forms, religious intolerance, and a disposition to violence; and that acquiesce in increasing illiteracy and reducing educational facilities in many countries. All this applies to every section of church and society.

We commit ourselves to create means by which the neglected and vulnerable may learn and the silenced may make themselves heard. We will seek to ensure that the truth, including the Word of God and accurate representation of other faiths, is communicated through modern media in imaginative, prophetic, liberating and respectful ways.

AFFIRMATION VI

We affirm the peace of Jesus Christ

The only possible basis for lasting peace is justice (Isaiah 32:17). The prophetic vision of peace with justice is this:

> "They shall beat their swords into ploughshares,
> and their spears into pruning hooks;
> nation shall not lift up sword against nation,
> neither shall they learn war any more;
> but they shall sit every[one]
> under [their] vine and fig tree,
> and none shall make them afraid;
> for the mouth of the Lord of hosts has spoken" (Micah 4:3-4).

Jesus said: "Blessed are the peacemakers" and "love your enemies". The church as the community of the crucified and risen Christ is called to perform a reconciling role in the world. We have to discern what it entails to be makers of peace: the conscious acceptance of vulnerability.

In Jesus Christ, God has broken through the bonds of hostility between nations and peoples, and even now offers us the gift of peace with justice. No wound, hostility or sinfulness is beyond the reach of the peace that passes understanding. For biblical faith, true peace means every human being dwelling in secure relatedness to God, neighbour, nature and self.

God's justice is to protect "the least" (Matthew 25:31-46), those who are the most vulnerable (Deuteronomy 24). God is the defender of the poor (Amos 5).

There can be no peace without justice. Such a peace cannot be obtained or guaranteed through narrowly conceived doctrines of national security, for peace is indivisible. True security must be based on justice for the people, especially for those most at risk, and on respect for the environment.

> We <u>affirm</u> the full meaning of God's peace. We are called to seek every possible means of establishing justice, achieving peace and solving conflicts by active non-violence.

> We <u>will resist</u> doctrines and systems of security based on the use of, and deterrence by, all weapons of mass destruction, and military invasions, interventions and occupations. We will resist doctrines of national security which are aimed at the control and suppression of the people in order to protect the privileges of the few.

> We <u>commit</u> ourselves to practice non-violence in all our personal relationships, to work for the banning of war as a legally recognized means of resolving conflicts, and to press governments for the establishment of an international legal order of peacemaking.

AFFIRMATION VII

We affirm the creation as beloved of God

As Creator, God is the source and sustainer of the whole cosmos. God loves the creation. Its mysterious ways, its life, its dynamism - all reflect the glory of its Creator. God's work of redemption in Jesus Christ reconciles all things and calls us to the healing work of the Spirit in all creation.

Because creation is of God and the goodness of God permeates all creation, we hold all life to be sacred. Today all life in the world, both present and future generations, are endangered because humanity has failed to love the living earth; and the rich and powerful in particular have plundered it as if it were created for selfish purposes. The magnitude of the devastation may well be irreversible and therefore forces us to urgent action.

Biblical statements, such as "to have dominion" and "subdue the earth", have been misused through the centuries to justify destructive actions toward the created order. As we repent of this violation, we accept the biblical teaching that people, created in the image of God, have a special responsibility as servants in reflecting God's creating and sustaining love, to care for creation and to live in harmony with it.

We affirm that the world, as God's handiwork, has its own inherent integrity; that land, waters, air, forests, mountains and all creatures, including humanity, are "good" in God's sight. The integrity of creation has a social aspect which we recognize as peace with justice, and an ecological aspect which we recognize in the self-renewing, sustainable character of natural ecosystems.

We will resist the claim that anything in creation is merely a resource for human exploitation. We will resist species extinction for human benefit; consumerism and harmful mass production; pollution of land, air and waters; all human activities which are now leading to probable rapid climate change; and policies and plans which contribute to the disintegration of creation.

Therefore we commit ourselves to be members of both the living community of creation in which we are but one species, and members of the covenant community of Christ; to be full co-workers with God, with moral responsibility to respect the rights of future generations; and to conserve and work for the integrity of creation both for its inherent value to God and in order that justice may be achieved and sustained.

AFFIRMATION VIII

We affirm that the earth is the Lord's

The land and the waters provide life to people - indeed, to all that lives - now and for the future. But millions are deprived of land and suffer from the contamination of waters. Their cultures, their spirituality and their lives are destroyed. Peoples indigenous to the land and its historical caretakers have particularly suffered and still suffer oppressive separation from their land - by government policy and by violence, by theft and deceit, and by cultural and physical genocide. They await the fulfilment of the promise for the meek to inherit the earth. When there is justice in the land, the fields and forests and every living thing will dance and sing for joy (Psalm 96:11-12). Therefore,

> We <u>affirm</u> that the land belongs to God. Human use of land and waters should release the earth to regularly replenish its life-giving power, protecting its integrity and providing spaces for its creatures.

> We <u>will resist</u> any policy that treats land merely as a marketable commodity; that allows speculation at the expense of the poor; that dumps poisonous wastes into the land and the waters; that promotes the exploitation, unequal distribution or contamination of the land and its products; and that prevents those who live directly from the land from being its real trustees.

> We <u>commit</u> ourselves to join in solidarity with indigenous communities struggling for their cultures, spirituality, and rights to land and sea; to be in solidarity with peasants, poor farmers and seasonal agricultural workers seeking land reform; and to have reverence for the ecological space of other living creatures.

AFFIRMATION IX

We affirm the dignity and commitment of the younger generation

Jesus actively upheld the dignity of the younger generation. His indication that unless we become like little children we cannot enter into the kingdom of God (Luke 18:17) and Paul's call to Timothy not to allow anyone to despise him because of his youth (I Timothy 4:12) implies a challenge to society to build human communities which, with wonder and curiosity, playfulness and vulnerability, with heart, soul and body, ensure the continuity of generations in the love of God. Poverty, injustice and the debt crisis, war and militarism, hit children hard through dislocation of families, forcing them into work at an early age just to survive, inflicting malnutrition upon them and even threatening their survival. Millions of children, particularly the girl child, have no security in order to enjoy their childhood. The increase in unemployment, especially among young people, causes despair. Therefore:

<u>We affirm</u> the dignity of children which derives from their particular vulnerability and need for nurturing love.

<u>We affirm</u> the creative and sacrificial role that the young people are playing in building a new society, recognizing their right to have a prophetic voice in the structures that affect their life and their community.

<u>We affirm</u> the rights and needs of the younger generation as basic for establishing educational and developmental priorities.

We <u>will resist</u> any policy or authority which violates the rights of the younger generation, and which abuses and exploits them. The human right of conscientious objection must be fully respected.

We <u>commit</u> ourselves to our responsibility to support young people in their struggle for self-actualization, participation, and a life of hope and faith; and to create conditions which enable all children to live in dignity, and where old and young share experiences and learn from each other.

AFFIRMATION X

We affirm that human rights are given by God

There is an inseparable relationship between justice and human rights. Human rights have their source in God's justice which relates to an enslaved, marginalized, suffering people in concrete acts of deliverance from oppression (Exodus 3:7b). We recognize with contrition that we as churches have not been in the forefront of the defence of human rights, and many times through our theology have justified human rights violations.

The term "human rights" must be clearly understood to refer not only to individual rights but also to the collective social, economic and cultural rights of peoples (including those with disabilities) such as the right to land and its resources, to one's own ethnic and racial identity and to the exercise of religious and political freedom. The right to sovereignty and self-determination for peoples to work out their own models of development and to live free of fear and free of manipulation is a fundamental human right which should be respected, likewise the rights of women and children to a life free of violence in home and society.

We <u>affirm</u> that human rights are God-given and that their promotion and protection are essential for freedom, justice and peace. To protect and defend human rights, an independent judicial system is necessary.

We <u>will resist</u> all structures and systems that violate human rights and deny the opportunity for the realization of the full potential of individuals and peoples. We will resist in particular torture, disappearances, and extra-judicial executions and the death penalty.

We <u>commit</u> ourselves to actions of solidarity with organizations and movements working for the promotion and protection of human rights; we will work for the acceptance and full implementation of human rights standards through effective instruments.

We further <u>commit</u> ourselves to work towards the full social integration of persons with disabilities into our communities through all possible means, including the removal of economic, religious, social and cultural barriers, (particularly ensuring access to buildings, documentation and information) which prevent them from fully participating in our communities.

Appendix IIIe.

"Chapter 12: Theological Issues," *Climate Change and the Quest for Sustainable Societies;* **Geneva: WCC Unit III, January 1998, pp. 38-41.**

THEOLOGICAL ISSUES

The challenges posed by the ecological crisis raise many theological issues. Theology has not naturally been an ally of the cause of sustainability. In many ways, theological thinking had contributed to and adapted itself to the ideological assumptions of Western culture discussed above. For some time now, the debate on the true Biblical witness has been under way. Themes connected with creation and the place of human beings in creation have come to the fore. We mention three issues that have been particularly important in our debate.

a) **Conquest or Communion?**

What is exactly the place of human beings before God and in relation to fellow-creatures? Scripture speaks of a special position before God. Humans are made in God's image and therefore singled out before all other creatures. What does this mean? Christians have long considered themselves as the crown of creation, the creatures most like God. This high calling, however, has not always or even usually meant a heightened sense of responsibility and appreciation for the rest of creation but rather an entitlement to use nature for human profit and pleasure.

A 1966 World Council of Churches statement expressed the following perspective:

> The biblical story...secularizes nature. It places creation - the physical world - in the context of covenant relation and does not try to understand it apart from that relation. The history of God with his people has a setting, and this setting is called nature. But the movement of history, not the structure of the setting, is central to reality. Physical creation even participates in this history; its timeless and cyclical character, as far as it exists, is unimportant. The physical world, in other words, does not have its meaning in itself.[17]

The Bible leaves no doubt that human beings, though they are made in God's image, are also part of creation and are summoned to live in communion with their fellow creatures. The balance between these two statements has not been preserved in recent centuries. Attention was paid ever more exclusively to the development of humanity as opposed to the rest of creation. God's history in relation to humanity rather than to the whole of creation was to the fore as a topic of theological interest. It was taken almost for granted that God had made the creation for the sake of human beings, and that God's work of redemption was focused on humanity. Theology, moreover, under the onslaught of natural sciences, increasingly withdrew into what was supposedly its own realm: the meaning and purpose of human existence. Creation, its coming to be and its goal, faded into the background. It was seen as the location where the drama between God and humankind was played out.

The monstrous effects of climate change, effects brought about by human mis-use of nature, are opening our eyes to who we really are. To be made in God's image does not mean that we are God's but rather God's ally, not God's darling but God's partner. Our calling is not to a place of privilege but to a place of responsibility. The sobering effects of climate change are a wake-up call to Christians to radically reconsider the place of human beings in the scheme of things. No longer can we continue ruining the planet like heedless children, expecting God to clean up after us. We are meant to be adults and the future of the earth is in our hands - not totally and perhaps not successfully, but more sub-stantially than we previously believed. We now know that what we do matters and knowing this, we cannot pretend we do not know or live as if we do not care.

Climate change not only makes us aware that we are responsible for the earth; it also makes us aware that we love it. The thought of a ruined planet, a planet unable to provide sustenance and joy for our children and grandchildren, makes us feel sad. We also begin to realize our sense of kinship with other life-forms and our desire to see them flourish. Loving the earth is preparation for a basic shift in sensibility for Christians: a conversion to the earth. Christians need a mind-shift, a heart-shift, to the earth and the well-being of all its creatures, human and non-human. The God who created the earth with all its wonderful creatures and who became incarnate in one of these creatures calls us to this conversion. The incar-nate One does not ask us to love God and despise the earth but to love God and live in communion with all creatures.

b) **Household and 'kindom'**

From the beginning the ecumenical movement has not been limited to unifying the churches but rather has been an attempt to gather the churches of the whole 'oikumene' to witness together to God's great deeds. Oikumene means the 'whole world'. In this meaning, it is not limited to Christians nor even to human beings but refers to the entire creation and all its creatures. Thus, conversion to the earth means that Christians should consider the entire earth as the household (oikos) of God. The traditional house in Africa, we were told at our consultation, is built in a circle - a round house as an image of the earth. The circular house in which we all live suggests something very important about how we should relate to one another within this household.

God's household can be understood as 'kindom' containing all God's creatures. Much of Western as well as Christian thinking has been patterned on a very different model, a dualist one: humans over nature, males over females, whites over people of colour, Northern countries over Southern ones, Christians over non-Christians. In this model relationship is hierarchical, with one species, gender, colour, country, or religion primary and all others inferior. But the circular household of earth gives a different model of relationship: an ecological one. In this model, all are profoundly interrelated and interdependent and at the same time radically individualized and diverse. We cannot live a day without the plants so deep is our dependence on them, but we are all, every human being and every plant, different from all the others. We do not have to be the same to be united; in fact, ecological unity is built on interdependent differences.

So, our household, our kindom, of earth is a vast, complex, interdependent, diverse, wondrous place created by God for the well-being of all its inhabitants. Who are we in this household? We are, first of all, members of the family, kin to all the others who live here. This household is our home, we belong here - we are neither aliens nor visitors. As made in God's image, we have been given special responsibilities for this household, for we are the ones, the only ones, who know its "house rules," the things we must do and not do in order to maintain a well-run home.

What must we do? Quite simply, we must learn to live by the rules in our home, God's household. Above all else, what climate change is telling us is that this household must be a sustainable community at every level, from planet-wide economics to family economics. "Economics," from the same word base (oikos) as ecumenism and ecology, means "the management of a household."

Economics, then, is a central Christian concern for it has to do with how the basic material needs of the household's members are met. Since the household includes all human members as well as all other life-forms (the entire kindom), Christians need to be inclusive in economic considerations. The abundant life that God calls us to can be neither an individual human being's salvation nor the current consumer version of well-being. Rather, it must be a <u>shalom</u> vision for the entire family of God's creatures.

But what, practically speaking, does this mean? It will mean different things for different peoples and creatures. Woven together as we are by bonds of interre-lationship and interdependence in this household of earth, we need not fear diversity. We need not seek <u>one</u> answer to the question, "What must we do?" but we will share our answers for the benefit of a common witness. Learning to live by the planet's house rules, by its proper economics, is a matter of induction, of piecing together stories and strategies of survival and flourishing from local com-munities, bio-regions, and citizens' efforts, as well as ecclesiastical initiatives and governmental legislation. The process will not be neat or simple. Rather, united by a common problem - the threat of climate change to our planet - we Christians, along with all others who want the earth to flourish, should work at various pieces of the planetary agenda.

For example, those people and countries that are responsible for most of the emissions that create climate change must do something different from those people and countries who are the principal recipients of the effects of the emis-sions. A word of judgment should be spoken to the elites of both the first and third worlds as well as a call for a radical change in their consumer lifestyle. These peo-ple are not loving the earth and its inhabitants; rather, they are casting an arro-gant eye on it, perceiving it to be theirs for the taking. They do not accept the intrinsic value either of other people or of other lifeforms: these others are simply "for" or "against" me and my kind. Christian witness, guided by the economic rules of the household of God, the rules that insist on providing basic needs for all family members, must denounce such outrageous greed. The new vision of who we are - members of God's kindom - requires us to demand an economics that can sustain the entire community.

c) **What can we hope for?**

Christian hope has often been individual and tribal: hope for one's own redemp-tion and for one's nearest and dearest. It has also been a "shalom" vision oriented to another world, one inhabited only by Christians. Our conversion to the earth (who we are) and our calling to work for the well-being of the entire household (what we must do), means that our hope changes as well. We do not hope just for eternal life in another world, but for a transformed life in this world. We hope for the kindom's well-being.

But what sort of hope are we justified in maintaining? There is a very deep conviction in western thought that human history is characterized by the march of progress. This belief has both infected and been reinforced by Christian theology. A document from the 1961 Assembly of the WCC states that "the Christian should welcome scientific discoveries as new steps in man's domination of nature"[18]. The pastoral constitution *Gaudium et Spes* of the Second Vatican Council expressed a general expectation that "…(human beings), created in God's image, received a mandate to subject (to themselves) the earth and all that it contains…thus, by the subjugation of all things to (humanity), the name of God would be wonderful in all the earth." [19]

From this viewpoint, it was the duty of the churches to follow this movement critically but above all constructively. Obstacles and even set-backs were to be expected. Nevertheless, Christians could start from the certainty that God would lead humanity over all the obstacles to the historical fulfilment God had intended. To be sure, God's kingdom lay beyond any kind of fulfilment within human history. But there was a connection between the ongoing course of history and ultimate fulfilment in the kingdom of God, for the forces of the kingdom were already at work in the history of humankind.

These considerations lead almost inevitably to the conclusion that human history will be "sustainable" in all circumstances. They supply the motivation for a critical militancy. They do not, however, take into account the possibility that the historical project to which humanity has been committed for decades can, as such, bear within itself the seeds of self-destruction. Accordingly, on the basis of these perspectives, it was difficult to make out the crisis at an early stage, for surely that would have called into question the achievements which we have celebrated as human progress for so many years.

The current hopes for the future, therefore, increasingly show themselves to be quite illusory. The ecological crisis makes us aware that self-destruction is a real possibility to be reckoned with. For theology to downplay the signs which point in this direction would be to turn itself into ideology. The only appropriate understanding of hope is one which integrates the signs of decay. The future is radically open. Hope which takes reality into account has to face the possibility of the failure and even the end of the human race. That does not mean that all hope must be abandoned. But real hope must rely on the conviction that the future is ultimately in God's hands - "for *yours* is the kingdom", as we say each time we recite the Lord's Prayer.

This does not mean surrendering to fatalism. The hope that ultimately all is in God's hands is a source of freedom. Precisely because it liberates us from the compulsion of the ideologies of growth and progress, it enables us to accept the challenge and to strike out on paths that at first sight look like steps backwards. Those who make their behaviour dependent on growth and success will soon be discouraged. The expectation of God's kingdom of love makes us capable of love even irrespective of the course finally taken by history. From one moment to the next, we shall stand up for the preservation of God's gift of life. What is involved here is something like an Hippocratic oath uniting the churches and to which they must be committed in view of the phenomena of disintegration and decay. It is a matter of opposing the destruction of life with commitment and forethought.

NOTES

[17]Granberg-Michaelson, Wesley, *Creation in Ecumenical Theology*, in *Ecotheology – Voices from South and North*, edited by David G. Hallman, WCC/Orbis, 1994, pg. 96.
[18]*Ibid*, p. 97.
[19]*Guadiem et Spes*, Second Vatican Council, § 34.

Appendix IIIf.

Rasmussen, Larry, "Sustainable Development and Sustainable Community: Divergent Paths," in *Development Assessed: Ecumenical Reflections and Actions on Development*, Geneva: WCC Unit III, 1995. Pp. 163-181.

SUSTAINABILITY

The centrepiece of the Earth Summit of 1992 was the notion of "sustainable development". It has since become common parlance for development talk and the substance of international agendas. Since the WCC may have given the world the currency of "sustainable" and "the sustainable society," it is noteworthy that the WCC has not spoken of "sustainable development". The thesis of this chapter is that this omission is telling and that the reason for it is the preference of the WCC for another path altogether, a path which might be named "sustainable community".

We take up WCC discussions first, in order to be clear about the acceptance, qualifications, or rejection by WCC participants of "sustainable development".

Shortly after the United Nations' Conference on the Environment in Stockholm, 1972, and for a 1974 conference in Bucharest on "Science and Technology for Human Development, The Ambiguous Future—The Christian Hope, a WCC statement introduced "sustainability" as a term applying to human behaviour and society. (This was in contrast with its earlier reference to renewable resources only, such as the "sustained yield" of forests and fisheries). The 1974 World Council statement gave sustainability human flesh.

> The goal must be a robust, sustainable society, where each individual can feel secure that his quality of life will be maintained or improved. We can already delineate some necessary characteristics of this enduring society. First, social stability cannot be obtained without an equitable distribution of what is in scarce supply and common opportunity to participate in social decisions. Second, a robust global society will not be sustainable unless the need for food is at any time well below the global capacity to supply it, and unless the emissions of pollutants are well below the capacity of the ecosystem to absorb them. Third, the new social organization will be sustainable only as

long as the rate of use of non-renewable resources does not outrun the increase in resources made available through technological innovation. Finally, a sustainable society requires a level of human activity which is not adversely influenced by the never ending, large and frequent natural variations in global climate.[1]

The next year, at Nairobi, the Council adopted a new programme - toward a "Just, Participatory, and Sustainable Society". Sustainability here is clearly a norm for society. Yet there was firm insistence that sheer sustainability was not of itself enough, as a norm. Or, rather, that "sustainable" should never be defined in ways which do not give equal normative emphasis to "just" and "participatory". Justice and participation were in fact the first characteristics listed in the 1974 statement (see above). While sustainability is ecological, it also includes transformation of present societal structures, systems and practices so as to render them sustainable in their own right. "If the life of the world is to be sustained and renewed,...it will have to be with a new sort of science and technology governed by a new sort of economics and politics," Charles Birch told the Nairobi Assembly.[2] "The rich must live more simply," he added, "that the poor may simply live".[3]

Sustainability thus encompasses not only the environment but all of earth's distress, including its human distress. Moreover, this scope has an explicit ethical focus. The moral dimensions are basic qualifiers and determinants, not what is considered only after development engines are in place and running full tilt. Nairobi meant to emphasize, and did, that "a sustainable society which is unjust can hardly be worth sustaining. A just society that is unsustainable is self-defeating."[4] Insistence of this scope and moral focus carries through like a strong pedal line in later WCC programmes as well, on "Justice, Peace, and the Integrity of Creation," "Ecumenical Decade of the Churches in Solidarity with Women," and "Theology of Life".

The ethical focus necessitated a certain kind of analysis - a critique of reigning socio-economic and political practices from a moral point of view. Viewing sustainability as an "ecological" term only, one might conclude, for example, that soil erosion and exhaustion undermining the agricultural base of society render it "unsustainable". Farming marginalized lands too intensively and neglecting adequate soil conservation would be the critical "eco" causes of sustainability.

But what causes the farming of marginalized lands? That may have been the result of marginalizing peasant farmers, driving them from better lands better used in the interests of export cropping for agribusiness and commerce in the globalised economy. These are socio-economic and political causes of ecological unsustainability. And they lead into or follow from questions about society as a just, participatory and sustainable society. They follow from a moral and ethical critique.

DEVELOPMENT

If "sustainability" has been a WCC theme since the 1970s, "development" has been for even longer. But development here refers to the appropriate technology and community development movements of the 1960s and 1970s, themselves born of dissatisfaction with the dominant form (mass economic growth led by rich industrial nations). E. F. Schumacher, himself an active friend of the Council, and his classic Small is Beautiful (1973) can be cited as influential sources, yet they were only reporting the experience, albeit brilliantly, that development as mass economic growth would invariably face environmental bottlenecks and did not in any case yield sustainable local communities with power to control or use their own native resources well.

There was a strong anti-capitalist anti-Western tone in much of this approach to development from the very beginning. In the Cold War context, development of this ilk was invariably construed by its many critics as Marxist and Communist or at least leftist. This cost the World Council and development organizations dearly.[5] But the fundamental point was not essentially socialist. It was that capitalist economics prosper most when labour, technology, and capital are fluid; they are thus driven to international integration at high levels; and this takes place at the expense of local communities, their resources, culture, and ways of life. The testimony was to capitalism as a "creative destruction" process (Schumpeter) in which destruction and benefits fell out very unevenly. And in a resource scarce world (where, to quote Boutros Boutros-Ghali at the Earth Summit, "progress is not necessarily compatible with life" and "the time of the finite world has come in which we are under house arrest")[6] the final result is that rich and poor end up in mortal competition for a dwindling resource base. The increasing poor increasingly lose.

Yet the WCC critique was not an economic one only. Global development bore a materialism and secularism that undermined and destroyed traditional ways and worldviews. Technical rationality and consumption as a way of life were not "advances" and "progress" at all, but forces that devalued local culture, work, technology, lifestyle, religion, philosophy, and social institutions. Ancient religious and cultural practices were rendered quaint, and age-old questions of ultimate means and purpose were not even considered significant matters of attention for "development". Spiritual vacuousness and homelessness set in, as did estrangement from the sacred and alienation from the earth. Loss of identity and cultural schizophrenia were common experiences, as were serious generational chasms in societies undergoing compressed change. No place felt like oikos - "home". Dislocation at several levels replaced "eco"-location.[7]

Such criticisms were voiced at meeting after meeting. Perhaps the sharpest of all came from Third World women and from indigenous peoples who had been on the receiving end of a deadly correlation far too long: the farther "development" penetrated, the more their culture *and* their environment were despoiled. The last thing they desired was to render all this "sustainable!"

Another criticism to the fore in World Council circles *was* an economic one. "Sustainable development" as a modified version of earlier development did nothing to change what many called the propensity of the global economy to create both "internal" and "external" "colonies". Nature, women, and the poor were just such colonies in many locales. This economic colonization was the mechanism for what can be called "*appropriated* carrying capacity," as now seen from the side of those from whom the appropriation took place. The charge they brought was that ongoing growth and prosperity for the well-off was sustained by externalizing the costs to communities elsewhere. If full economic, environmental and social costs had instead been *internalized within* the centres of benefit (wealthier nations and wealthy sectors of poor nations) there would have been a quick end to claims about the glory and beauty of growth. In short, this was the economics of borrowing and appropriating as reported by those who were squeezed, even crushed, rather than sustained.

Little of this would change, the criticism went on (sometimes *ad nauseam*), so long as basic changes in trade, debt, and aid were not forthcoming and so long as sustainable development policies were marginal to the basic economic policy-making decisions of government, business, and finance, a criticism borne out in efforts since Rio.[8]

"Sustainability," whether attached to "development" or "society," has thus come to mean something very different in WCC and other NGO circles from its prevailing notion in UN, business, and nation-state circles North and South. It means, *not* global economic growth qualified by environmental sensitivity, but local and regional communities that are economically viable, socially equitable, and ecologically renewable. Earth itself in these locales is part of their very sense of being. It is their habitat, their patch of *oikos*, "home".

The search, therefore, is for local and regional self-reliance and economic and environmental sustainability. The approach is usually a basic needs approach, with poverty eradication as a major goal. Since poverty eradication and meeting basic needs are also goals of the United Nations and the World Commission on Environment and Development (popularly known as the Brundtland Commission), the difference of approach may not be readily apparent. Differences are further masked by a common vocabulary now of "community development," "empowerment," "grassroots participation," etc. But the differences are recognized concurrently with the realization that for this to happen, a *sufficiency* revolution (redistributed power and access in society and between societies) is as important as an *eco-efficiency* one (more environmentally benign technologies and production). And the two belong together. "Healthy" eco-efficient business isn't enough. In fact, under conditions of fierce competition, healthy, eco-efficient business might of itself generate high employment and send manufacturing down the very same track as agriculture. (What was once the largest U.S. employer - agriculture - now feeds itself and more with only 2 or 3% of the work force.)[9] In a small world doubling its population, eco-efficiency and other technical solutions are therefore insufficient. Sustainability requires equity, and the first step toward equity is to transfer resources from non-essential to essential consumption, a transfer from wasteful wants to irreducible needs.

Yet even sufficiency as a norm did not complete the WCC critique. The theme of "participation," from Nairobi with its programme of a "Just, Participatory, and Sustainable Society" to the present, has consistently meant a community focus for decision-making that considers the "local" as the basic unit of the "global" in economic life. The 1992 WCC study document, <u>Christian Faith and the World Economy Today</u>, goes so far as to say that these issues of participation lead to "possibly the most crucial question of all in this paper" (i.e., the study document itself). That question is then posed: "in a world increasingly divided between those who can decide what life will be like for themselves and for others, and those who can only submit to what others have arranged and provided for them, how can we move towards systems which give all people(s) a genuine share in reaching the decisions that affect their lives?"[10] Differently said, an abstract equity isn't enough either if it sidesteps peoples' hands-on participation in the crucial decisions impacting their communities and thus their lives.

AN ECUMENICAL APPROACH

We can illustrate all this with two documents, both of them conscientious responses to Earth Summit issues. One is a WCC document prepared by representatives from around the world entitled "Accelerated Climate Change: Sign of Peril, Test of Faith". In addition to illustrating the community alternative to sustainable development, it reflects the WCC theme, "the integrity of creation," and its implicit ethic. The other document is the Report of the Secretary-General of the United Nations, "An Agenda for Development". This is not a statement of the Secretary-General's personal views, however, but his mandated task to "gather the widest range of views about the topic of development"... "from all Member States, as well as the agencies and programmes of the United Nations system"[11] and offer them to the General Assembly for UN policy deliberation. Secretary-General Boutros Boutros-Ghali's report comes two years after the Earth Summit and may said to represent fairly widespread views among international representatives of nations and transnational organizations. Our purpose here is to compare and contrast the WCC and UN documents as a way of highlighting different approaches to sustainability and sustainable development.

Turning first to the WCC paper, the Introduction to "Accelerated Climate Change: Sign of Peril, Test of Faith" moves quickly to the ethical issues: "Accelerated climate change represents not only a threat to life but also an inescapable issue of justice. It throws into sharp relief the unjust balance of wealth, resources and economic power between the rich and poor that characterizes the world today." (p. 7) After marshalling data about global warming and its sources, an argument for policy is made on the grounds of justice. An example is this one.

From the Christian perspective, the setting of targets cannot be dissociated from the intensifying issues of social and economic justice. The global economy presents a picture of gross inequality: an affluent minority of the world's people lives in the North, an impoverished majority lives in the South. Extreme inequalities also exist within both North and South. The industrial way of life promotes material consumption far beyond actual need. It is undeniable that this way of life has precipitated the greenhouse effect. In this context we need to question seriously the prevailing model of development...Targets for the North must go beyond limiting emissions through various technological fixes, to questions of new lifestyles based on conservation, renewable energy and equitable resource distribution. Targets for the South will centre on the formulation and implementation of new development models that reject the destructive path of Northern industrial development and recognize the imperatives of social equity and ecological sustainability.[12]

One conclusion drawn is that "in this crisis, compounded in the violation of intricate natural systems and the disruptive exploitation of vulnerable human communities, nature has become co-victim with the poor. Earth and people will be liberated to thrive together, or not at all."[13]

This said and some ethical insights drawn,[14] the paper proceeds with analysis of "current political socio-economic realities." It affirms eco-efficiency but not within the dominant solution of greatly enhanced economic growth: "Using resources more efficiently in a world of ever-expanding material production and consumption only delays the inevitable. While producing more efficient automobiles is an important step, all reductions in petroleum consumption will eventually be cancelled out if the total number of automobiles continues to rise."[15] The eventual conclusion is that "[w]e are pushed to go beyond efficiency, renewable energy technologies and individual lifestyle changes to the formidable task of reconceiving and transforming the economic system. This task belongs within the context of a renewed vision of community."[16]

That said, the next chapter is "Building Community". The heart of it is a set of "ethical claims" (a.- e.) brought to bear "on economics". The chapter is introduced with a paragraph reminiscent of earlier WCC discussions of <u>oikos</u>.

> "Economy" in its Greek-root meaning is simply the ordering of the household for the sustenance of its members. Economy signifies the arrangements that people make in a household- or a community - or a community of communities- to draw sustenance from nature to meet their needs and wants. In accordance with Gen. 2:15, it signifies the work that humans do to "till the garden" but also to "keep" it so that the tilling may continue. The ordering of work for the sake of life belongs to God's purpose for human beings and the whole creation. As such, it falls under God's will and intention that love-as-justice be expressed in the structures, policies, and practices of economics.[17]

The ethical claims on economics then follow.

> a. <u>Ecological sustainability</u>. Economics must come to terms with the ecological realities that make endless material growth unsustainable. The claim of sustainability, however, must transcend anthropocentric self-interest. Without a sense of awe and reverence before the goodness and grandeur of the whole created order, humans will not likely preserve their habitat.
>
> b. <u>Sufficiency of sustenance</u>. A majority of the people in the South and a significant minority in the North need more access to energy, work, and land in order to obtain sufficient sustenance. Human-enhanced climate change gives this claim on economics a distinctively contemporary twist: the folly of wasteful consumption, the urgent need for a sense of "enough" based on a less materialistic conception of the good life, and the responsibility of the comfortable and the wealthy to lighten their demand upon Earth's bounty so that it may provide enough for all.
>
> c. <u>Community through work</u>. This claim requires economics to regard people, not simply as individuals, but as persons-in-community. For enterprises to contribute constructively to genuine community, they have to exhibit concern for the well-being of their personnel, the environment and their consumers as an intrinsic part of their economic mandate. Work should involve people in satisfying relationships with co-workers. All work, all economic arrangements, should be conducive to community well-being.
>
> d. <u>Participation by all</u>. Participation means both the right and the responsibility to share in work for individual and family livelihood and the common good of the community. This makes unacceptable the situations that prevails today, in both South and North, where millions of people have been made superfluous non-participants in economic activity. The Christian recognition of human dignity requires that economics become more democratic, that people rightfully participate in decisions pertaining to their work and the kind of development that is best for their community.
>
> e. <u>Respect for diversity</u>. While the need for community is universal, communities are far from identical in their definitions of the common good or in their needs and wishes pertaining to development. A global economy must encompass and respect a wide variety of local, national, and regional communities.[18]

From the ethical claims for economic life, the paper moves to "Strategies for an Economy to Build Community" with several proposals for economic re-visioning and action.

a) Shift from unneeded production to work that needs to be done. There are massive employment possibilities in work that would address major unmet needs, including housing, healthcare, public transportation, environmental restoration, recreational, cultural, aesthetic opportunities that would enhance life for everyone. This is a challenge that market economics by itself cannot meet, since reliance upon unlimited economic growth is no longer tenable. We need creative planning leading to new policies, by governments and NGOs at many levels from the local community on up.

b. Make development increasingly community-based, focused on essential needs and the sustainable, equitable use of natural resources. Alternative kinds of development are being tried in many places, in both South and North. These entail local community organization and development, with an emphasis on participation by all members of the community in determining development goals, methods and technologies. The intention is to apply local resources more directly to local needs, to maintain or restore community support systems, and to reduce dependence upon outside forces and unstable commodity markets. Such development increases the capacity of communities to take care of their own most essential needs and makes trade more relevant to meeting those needs. Larger economic units or entities - regions, nations, international agencies - would increasingly construe their role as enabling their sub-components to be as self-reliant as realistically possible as well as maximally conserving of resources. This is a model that is much less energy-intensive - less prone to substitute mechanization for human labour than that which now prevails.

c. Organize and mobilize democratically to curb excessive power and empower all people. Political mobilization in South and North is critical. Churches and other non-governmental organizations have a key role to play in bringing about national policies and international cooperation that can meet the challenge of global warming, nurture community, and serve the cause of economic justice. Strong citizens' coalitions to monitor public policy and business practices are the best antidote to the corruption and the domination by special interests that now violate the common good.[19]

The conclusion of "Building Community" is also a question.

The transformation for which we call is already beginning in many places around the world as people struggle and organize to achieve their aspirations. What will the churches do to support localities, nations, and the world in moving towards economic and political arrangements that accommodate reduced consumption, promote new development models and nurture community? The answer will be a test of faith.[20]

THE UNITED NATIONS' APPROACH

Turning next to the United Nations' "Agenda For Development," "the dimensions of development" are listed as follows in the Table of Contents:

A. Peace as the foundation
B. The economy as the engine of progress
C. The environment as a basis for sustainability
D. Justice as a pillar of society
E. Democracy as good governance[21]

Most helpful for comparison are items B. and C., but D. will be touched upon as well.

Section B, "The economy as the engine of progress," begins as follows: "Economic growth is the engine of development as a whole. Without economic growth, there can be no sustained increase in household or government consumption, in private or public capital formation, in health, welfare and security levels."[22] The supporting paragraphs essentially echo the argument of the Brundtland report and the Business Council for Sustainable Development:

> Accelerating the rate of economic growth is a condition for expanding the resource base and hence for economic, technological and social transformation. While economic growth does not ensure that benefits will be equitably distributed or that the physical environment will be protected, without economic growth the material resources for tackling environmental degradation will not exist, nor will it be possible to pursue social programmes effectively in the long term. The advantage of economic growth is that it increases the range of human choice. It is not sufficient, however, to pursue economic growth for its own sake. It is important that growth be sustained and sustainable. Growth should promote full employment and poverty reduction, and should seek improved patterns of income distribution through greater equality of opportunity.[23]

Of additional note is the Secretary-General's statement that in the quest for sustained and sustainable economic growth, "governments can no longer be assumed to be paramount economic agents. They nonetheless retain the responsibility to provide a regulatory framework for the effective operation of a competitive market system."[24]

"The environment as a basis for sustainability," Section C, leads to the clearest differences with the WCC document and *oikos* community development. At most every point - the separation of environment and humanity, with the latter as managers, the view of nature and its subordination to economic ends, the uncritical affirmation of progress, and, like Brundtland, the wholly anthropocentric view of the existence of otherkind - the differences can be seen in but a few paragraphs.

> Development and environment are not separate concepts, nor can one be successfully addressed without reference to the other. The environment is a resource for development... Successful development requires policies that incorporate environmental considerations. This link was accepted at the United Nations Conference on Environment and Development in 1992. That Conference provided a model for other efforts toward greater coherence in development. Preserving the availability and rationalizing the use of the earth's natural resources are among the most compelling issues that individuals, societies and States must face. A country's natural resources are often its most easily accessible and exploitable development assets. How well these natural resources are managed and protected has a significant impact on development and on a society's potential for progress.[25]

The next paragraph discloses the fundamentally anthropocentric and utilitarian nature of development in this scheme: "Environmental degradation reduces both the quality and the quantity of many resources used directly by people."[26] What then follows is an enumerated listing of various kinds of degradation with the negative consequences enumerated. All are judged by outcome for humans only. There is one sentence in another section about "the intrinsic worth and value of nature". But even it is raised in the context of the "tangible and material aspects of the environment" for social welfare and offers the pleasures of nature as an aesthetic good for society.[27]

"Community involvement in all development efforts" is a subject mentioned only in passing as well, though its importance is stated and "pioneering initiatives" of community groups applauded. The language is again telling, however. "By making local inhabitants incentive partners rather than simply collateral beneficiaries, these programmes have broken new ground."[28] The programmes of these "incentive partners" have led to "greater community cooperation in preserving tourist assets and higher rural incomes. They are examples from which many others can learn and benefit."[29] "Sustainable tourism strategies" are singled out as one concrete means for "preserving the natural environment".[30]

All this makes clear that what needs to be sustained, according to this model for sustainability, is "economic activity in the long term"[31] and that sustainable development means economic activity as qualified by environmental considerations in such a way as to secure sustainable economic growth. The Secretary-General is also clear that "at present, economic policy coordination among the major economies centres on the Group of Seven industrialized countries" (United States, Japan, Britain, France, Germany, Italy and Canada) but that it should be more broad-based.[32] Quite surprisingly, he accepts a human construct as fixed natural law itself and focuses change elsewhere: "The laws of economics cannot be changed, but their social consequences can be eased."[33] Presumably, broadening the base of policy coordination would aid this.

Other sections of the report stress the importance of social instability. "Poverty, resource degradation and conflict" are becoming "an all too familiar triangle" that raises the spectre of both waves of refugees and resource-based wars.[34] This underscores the need for, and reality of, "justice as a pillar of society".

The justice-and-security argument is made in terms consistent with what has gone before. "While investment in physical capital is an important aspect of stimulating economic growth, investment in human development is an investment in long-term competitiveness and a necessary component of stable and sustainable progress. Investment in human resources must, therefore, be seen not merely as a by-product of economic growth, but rather as a powerful and necessary driving force for all aspects of development. A stable economy and a stable political order cannot be built in an unstable society. A strong social fabric is a prerequisite to sustainability."[35]

We might add the similarity of this United Nations' picture of sustainable development to the World Bank's. The 50th anniversary of the World Bank in 1994 brought a broad review, including stinging criticism. In response a restatement of its vision was part of the anniversary event. Entitled "Embracing the Future," the president, Lewis Preston, enumerated five basic challenges for the bank: promoting broad-based economic growth that particularly benefits the poor; stimulating private sectors so developing countries can be more competitive in the global economy; reorienting governments to become more efficient at complementing the private sector; protecting the environment; and investing more in human development programmes supporting education, nutrition, family planning, and the role of women.[36]

DEVELOPMENT AND ECONOMIC GROWTH

Perhaps this suffices to contrast the approaches as well as note agreement that "a strong social fabric is a prerequisite to sustainability". All that remains is to cite remaining arguments from the World Council, some NGOs and people's movements, against the dominant notion of sustainable development and its realization by various transnational organizations. These go beyond the United Nations and include the World Bank and many transnational corporations and NGOs.

The arguments where differences are greatest - on the relationship of economy and ecology - are essentially two. The economics of the reigning approach to sustainable development is bad economics, in World Council view. And its rendering of the good society and sustainability is too "economistic".

Too "economistic" means that social well-being is measured by rising or falling Gross National Product (GNP). Of course for millions of destitute people, to *have* more *is* required in order to *be* more. Championing socio-economic equity and bending the market to address basic needs has thus been an unrelenting theme of the World Council and many NGOs in community development work. But once people are above the poverty line, there is very little correlation of happiness and well-being with increased consumption and rising incomes. Satisfactions in life relate more closely to the quality of family life and friendships, work, leisure, and spiritual richness. None of these are well measured by GNP. In fact, in societies with the highest levels of consumption, where the basic choice of serving God or mammon has been faced squarely and decided in favour of the latter hands down, there seems to be an inordinate psychological and spiritual emptiness. (Which then commerce plies in order to sell more goods and services for greater self-fulfilment!)

But development as economic growth is not only too economistic, it is bad economics as well. Basically the criticism of the WCC, many NGOs and people's movements, is this: domestic and global wealth is generated without eradicating poverty or making local communities more viable and sustainable.

The argument, somewhat differently put, is that the high level efforts of the eco-sensitive Brundtland Commission, the Business Council for Sustainable Development, and *Agenda 21* cannot attain their own good ends because the means fail them. The numbers just don't work. Official sustainable development counts on environmentally safe economic growth to alleviate poverty, rather than attempting the much more politically difficult path of socio-economic redistribution. To this end Brundtland targets a 3 percent annual growth in income. But economists at the World Bank, in a working paper entitled "Building on Brundtland," show the following results:

> [A]n annual 3% global rise in per capita income translates initially into annual per capita income increments of $633 for USA; $3.6 for Ethiopia; $5.4 for Bangladesh; $7.5 for Nigeria; $10.8 for China and $10.5 for India. By the end of ten years, such growth will have raised Ethiopia's per capital income by $41.0..."etc.[37]

Former World Bank President Robert McNamara had earlier observed that, because of the gap in real income between rich and poor nations, "Even if the growth rate of the poor countries doubled, only seven would close the gap with the rich nations in 100 years. Only another nine would reach our level in 1000 years."[38]

Conclusion? Growth does not eliminate poverty.

Worldwatch Institute offers other longer-term corroborating evidence. *State of the World 1990*, in its overview entitled "The Illusion of Progress," notes that on average the additions to global economic output during *each* of the last four decades matched economic growth from the beginning of civilization to 1950! Yet during the same decades the ranks of the destitute soared. The World Bank puts the number of the "bottom billion" at 1.2 billion in 1990 and says these people scrape together a dollar a day or less per capita. The global rich number about the same as the destitute and include all middle strata as well as well as the upper strata of Northern nations. The 3.6 billion between are the "managing" poor. They do more than exist but do not live well or without fear. The ranks of both the destitute and the managing poor are almost certain to grow in coming decades, even with 3% annual economic growth. Too, these same four decades of unprecedented economic growth saw environmental destruction grow alarmingly. Since mid-century the world has lost nearly one fifth of cropland topsoil, a fifth of the tropical forests, and thousands of plant and animal species. The rending of the social fabric has proceeded apace during this boom time as well.[39]

The numbers get worse when growth is tracked by "developed" and "developing" sectors. Inequality between and within societies accompanies high growth rates. The share of total world production in developing countries a century ago was 44%. By 1950 it was 17%! It recovered to 20-21% by 1980, still less than half what it was the century earlier. By this time, however, (1980) the developing world's population share was about 75-80% and counting.[40] This means that 20-25% of the world's population, the advanced industrial countries, contributes 80% of world production.

Conclusion? "Catching-up development" is not working.

Nonetheless, the Brundtland Report's recommendation is a 5 - 10 times increase in world output, as stimulated by the North, in order to meet the objective of poverty reduction everywhere. This must be done without increasing environmental degradation, and in fact reversing much of it.[41]

Two comments almost write themselves in response to what crunching the numbers shows for the reigning model of sustainable development and its plan of action for sustainability. The first is that persons often regarded as consummate, worldly realists - business people, economists, politicians and diplomats - show themselves here to be pure utopians in the pejorative sense; they are dreamers with no place to stand on the solid ground of sound evidence. Schmidheiny's earlier admission that for the moment, merging economic growth and environmental sustainability is a dream, turns out to be even more "ecomystical" than he himself likely suspected. His hope, and that of sustainable development on the going model, is hallucinatory. The second comment is that the approach itself is backwards, given its own objectives. The argument is that governments and societies need not limit economic growth so long as they stabilize use of natural resources. They will in fact need to increase growth dramatically (Brundtland) while achieving stabilization through the second industrial revolution of eco-efficiency. But why not, as per Lele, turn the matter around and suggest that if economic growth is not correlated with environmental sustainability, then there is no reason to have economic growth as an objective of sustainable development. If the reply (a good one) is that economic growth is absolutely necessary to remove poverty, then the question is why it has not done so, especially during boom decades when environmental constraints were little imposed? The question is why reviving growth is the first-listed objective of the Brundtland report and the object of the first substantial chapter of *Agenda 21* (chp. 2) if economic growth of itself leads neither to environmental sustainability nor removal of poverty? Why not consider the converse, as Lele suggests, and explore "whether successful implementation of policies for poverty removal, long-term employment generation, environmental restoration and rural development will lead to growth in GNP, and...to increases in investment, employment and income generation?[42] This would seem especially promising in the South, where it is most needed.

This brings to a close contrasting approaches to sustainability and its meaning. One begins with economies and their growth, the other with communities and theirs. For the former, sustainability for sustainable development belongs to those for whom the environment (*and* sustainability) are around their economies. For the latter, sustainability for sustainable community belongs to those for whom the environment (and sustainability) are around their homes (*oikos*).[43] That is, for sustainable development advocates, "sustainable" seems essentially a qualifier of the prevailing development path and largely assumes both its structure and its economistic ethic. And the issue its critics pose so sharply is whether sustainable development is any more than an environmentally-qualified continuation of the trek of post-World War II industrially-based economic growth, rather than quite another path altogether, as Brundtland and most delegates to the Earth Summit seemed to hope. Is sustainability here not "the ecologisation of world society" as "the latest version of Western development dynamics,"[44] a kind of "green globalism?"

Differently said, Brundtland, *Agenda 21*, and the Business Council for Sustainable Development all hope to bend an international global economic order in ways that make "poverty removal, long-term employment generation, environmental restoration and rural development" (Lele's list) the prime determinants of economic polity, policy, and practice. If they were, Brundtland et al. must know, the basic dynamics of the economic system itself would be fundamentally transformed. By contrast, the World Council and other members of a growing international civil society are sceptical in the extreme. In their judgment the international global economy has no intention of going this direction. If it does change course, it will be because its own ills require harsh treatment that must be undergone in order to prevent its own demise. In any case, sustainable development of this sort [read: unsustainable mal-development] is not what a restless and fragmented but vibrant international civil society is hoping and working for; namely, the break-up of both traditional economic domination *and* green globalism in favour of an ecumenism focused on viable communities, one which includes a careful consideration of (necessary) economic growth.

[1] Cited from *Study Encounter* 69, vol. X, no. 4, 1974, 2.

[2] Cited by Dieter T. Hessel, "Sustainability in Social Ethical Perspective," Paper for MIT Working Session, Feb. 13-14, 1994, p. 1 of unpublished manuscript.

[3] Also cited by Hessel, "Sustainability in Social Ethical Perspective," 1.

[4] From Nairobi report, "Social Responsibility in a Technological Age." Here taken from Dieter T. Hessel, "Sustainability in Social Ethical Perspective," 1.

[5] In the case of the WCC, the costs came via both internal controversy among member churches and through broad media exposure and condemnation in such as *The Reader's Digest,* a segment on *60 Minutes,* and Ernest Lefevre's *From Amsterdam to Nairobi.*

[6] As cited by Wesley Granberg-Michaelson, *Redeeming the Creation,* 6-7.

[7] The terms "dislocation" and "ecolocation" are Daniel Spencer's. See "The Liberation of Gaia," *Union Seminary Quarterly Review,* Vol. 47, Nos. 1-2, 1993, 91-102. I use "ecolocation" differently from Spencer, however, in keeping with earlier discussion of *oikos* as a vision. My use is normative, Spencer's descriptive.

[8] Only $2 billion over three years has been pledged for objectives that government heads meeting in Rio agreed will cost some $600 billion annually. Significant here is the additional fact that national ministers of economy and development are not even involved in the UN process. Rather, ministers of environment are sent, without the backing of financial and business interests as channelled through government representation or private. See "Panel Finds Lag in Saving Environment," *New York Times,* 29 May 1994, 13.

[9] This is not to argue that U.S. agriculture is a paragon of eco-efficiency. It is not! This is only to argue that businesses seeking eco-efficiency, under capitalist conditions, will, by way of efficient technology, likely shed employees in the pursuit of productivity; this, rather that generate humanly labour-intensive work.

[10] *Christian Faith and the World Economy Today* (Geneva: WCC Publications, 1992), 33.

[11] "An Agenda for Development: Report of the Secretary-General," Preface, 3.

[12] *Accelerated Climate Change,* 20.

[13] *Accelerated Climate Change,* 13.

[14] See pp. 13-14 of *Accelerated Climate Change.*

[15] *Accelerated Climate Change,* 23.

[16] *Accelerated Climate Change,* 24.

[17] *Accelerated Climate Change,* 26.

[18] "*Accelerated Climate Change,*" 26.

[19] "Building Community," *Accelerated Climate Change: Sign of Peril, Test of Faith,* 26-27.

[20] "Building Community," *Accelerated Climate Change,* 27.

[21] United Nations, "Agenda for Development: Report of the Secretary-General to the Forty-eighth Session of the General Assembly," Table of Contents.

[22] "Agenda for Development," 9.

[23] "Agenda for Development," 10.

[24] "Agenda for Development," 10.

[25] "Agenda for Development," 14.

[26] "Agenda for Development," 14.

[27] "Agenda for Development," 14-15.

[28] "Agenda for Development," 15.

[29] "Agenda for Development," 15.

[30] "Agenda for Development," 15.

[31] "Agenda for Development," 13.

[32] "Agenda for Development," 12.

[33] "An Agenda for Development," 20.

[34]"Agenda for Development," 17.

[35]"Agenda for Development," 19.

[36]"World Bank, At 50, Vows To Do Better," *New York Times*, 24 July 1994, A4.

[37]Cited by Korten, "Sustainable Development," *World Policy Journal*, 167, from Robert Goodland, Herman Daly, and Salah El Serafy, eds., "Environmentally Sustainable Economic Development: Building on Brundtland," working paper (Washington, DC: Environment Department, World Bank, July 1991), 6.

[38]McNamara as cited by Hawken, *The Ecology of Commerce*, 135. Hawken does not give the source.

[39]Lester R. Brown, "The Illusion of Progress," *State of the World 1990* (New York and London: W. W. Norton & Co., 1990), 3-4.

[40] Shridath Ramphal, *Our Country, The Planet: Forging a Partnership for Survival* (Washington, DC: Island Press, 1992), 147-148.

[41]For more discussion than space here allows, see *Christian Faith and the World Economy Today*, especially p. 18 ff., "The growing gap between rich and poor."

[42]Lele, "Sustainable Development: A Critical Review," *World Development*, 614.

[43]I am keenly aware of the deficiencies of using a two-term typology: development qualifiers and development dissenters, sustainable development and sustainable community. There are important groupings within each and the loyalties and work of many individuals and organizations intersect both. Sustainable development camps, for example, parallel virtually all the variants on capitalism, from something close to eco-attentive laissez-faire to welfare-state capitalism. Yet all of them, as indicated above, move into sustainability from within global capitalist economic frameworks and considerations, i.e., economic growth on a free market model. Development dissenters are even more varied, in part because most all of them begin with and focus on local issues. Thus Love Canal toxins and health issues create one kind of movement in resistance against government and industry in New York State, mining and logging and cattle ranching in tropical forest lands of indigenous peoples in the Amazon region another, and sewage treatment, a huge city bus terminal, and lines of idling garbage trucks for the Upper West Side off-loading onto barges, all nearby a grade school in Harlem, yet another. Nonetheless, this diversity shares the general characteristics of community approaches to sustainability outlined above.

[44]The phrases are Guy Beney's in "'Gaia': The Globalitarian Temptation," *Global Ecology*, 181.

Appendix IIIg.

Larry Rasmussen, "Theology of Life and Ecumenical Ethics", *Working on Theology of Life: A Dossier*; Geneva: WCC Unit III, 1998, pp. 12-24.

Ada Maria Isasi-Diaz and Yolanda Tarango helpfully sketch theology's task:

> It is unacceptable to speak of Theology (with a capital T) as if there were only one true way to deal with questions of ultimate meaning. Theology is... acceptable only as a heuristic device that provides a "space" in which different theologies can meet to discuss their commonalities and differences in order to deepen their understanding. This conversation is an important one for the different theologies to engage in because the struggles to which they relate are interconnected.[1]

This paper treats theology as the "space" Isasi-Diaz and Tarango call for. It cannot and does not wish to substitute for the vital reflection of faith emanating directly from churches and movements engaged in inter-local, intra-local and international struggles. It does not claim or aspire to be a theological package which need only be "applied" or "contextualized" in order to serve different locales. Theologies that are not local are not real, just as an ethic that is not somebody's is nobody's. The theology here, instead, gathers recent ecumenical themes and with them offers an articulated space for the "Theology of Life" initiative which the World Council of Churches has embarked upon as part of its follow-up of the Justice, Peace and Integrity of Creation (JPIC) process. With discussion and improvement, it might outline a coherent framework for varied theologies of life as these find voice through the interconnected struggles that have shaped our lives in recent and tumultuous decades.

THE FORMATIVE BIBLICAL STRANDS

The theological-ethical lines of the Hebrew Bible take their cues from the character and presence of God. This God, unlike many others in the god-rich world of the ancient Near East, was not recognized as simply a power or force in the universe which transcended human powers and suffused all nature with its energy. Rather, this sacred power was a moral force that rejected the inevitability of oppression and injustice and commanded and made possible transformation of the world on the terms of community. Community and social justice were the focus of biblical faith at the very outset.

Hebrew conviction about this godly power included a very strong ethical component: we are morally responsible before God for the condition of the world. In the ancient world, where forces outside and beyond the control of human beings bore down from all sides, this was an extraordinary affirmation of human agency and freedom. It was the claim, set down near the beginnings of the recorded human adventure itself, that co-participation with God in creation is the human vocation! Few claims about God could have contrasted more sharply with cultures and religious traditions which pictured life as subject to great uncontrollable powers. These reigning powers — sometimes embodied in human forms and offices, sometimes in the forces of nature, sometimes in spirits and gods and goddesses — needed to be appeased, submitted to, prayed to, feared. For the vast majority, life was essentially fated.

That the God of the Hebrews was power for transformation towards a moral order in which humans played an important role was grounded in the people's own transformation. The God who "knew" the suffering of slaves and heard their cries was the God whose power was experienced as the power for peoplehood and freedom. This God created a people from a ragtag band who were no people. This God hewed a way where there was none.

This same God, these ex-slaves came to believe, held this new people responsible for the shape and condition of the community and world that was theirs. Their vocation as a "redeemed" and "saved" people

In short, the governing power of the universe was not experienced or understood in the first instance as the principle of order and necessity — that might sum up fate and pharoah quite well! — but the principle of freedom and responsible moral agency.

What began with Moses and the first recorded slave rebellion soon becomes, in the biblical account, a paradigm of liberation and transformation as a way of life. "A way of life" is, in fact, the heart of the Hebrew and Jewish endeavour (and early Christian as well). This way is always an ethic inferred from the character and presence of the righteous and compassionate one who showed them mercy. Yet the specific point at the moment is the conviction that with this God, ordinary people — indeed, the apparently powerless — can subvert deeply entrenched powers and help effect a new world. In Michael Lerner's words, Judaism was "not just a religion about how wonderful the physical world is but a religion that insisted there is nothing inevitable about the hierarchies of the social world".[2]

Jesus and his movement maintained the outrageously hopeful Jewish conviction that with this God new creation can happen at the waiting hands of a small number of very common, even hesitant, but emboldened and Spirit-filled people. Drawing chiefly on the early Christian readings of the Genesis creation stories, Elaine Pagels has shown that until the time of Augustine and Constantine the gospel itself is understood in terms of extraordinary freedom and agency for creating new community (in this case amidst a dying culture and epoch, a "passing age").[3]

At the same time, Judaism was also what Lerner calls "a religion about how wonderful the physical world is". The liberating God was the creator of the universe itself. Thus the Hebrew Bible again and again celebrates the immense grandeur of creation, gives thanks for the breath of life that animates all creation — it is nothing less than the ongoing presence of the same Spirit which brooded over the waters of first creation — and marvels at the detail of a gracious God's good creation, knowing that Wisdom herself has been present from the beginning. A universal moral order is to be discerned in creation, it is claimed. Humans, while occupying a special place of power and responsibility within the orderings of life, ought properly to stand in awe of this universe, respect and learn from it, and humbly remember that like all earth creatures from *adamah* (earth, soil, ground), they too will return there.[4]

The salient matter, however, is that these biblical themes weave a single strand: the power that created the universe and sustains it from day to day is the same power that "champions the powerless and creates the demand for a moral universe infused with justice and compassion".[5] Psalm 77 is a striking example of this double theme becoming a single one, moving almost unconsciously between the ways of God as creator and as redeemer/liberator. Yet the psalmist does not begin in praise, but in despondency, hardly able to speak. Racked by the world's troubles and fearful that the Ancient of Days has forgotten to be gracious and has exchanged compassion for searing anger, the psalmist reaches deep to remember the character of this God of Exodus and to confess in awe, fear, and gratitude, despite feeling all the weight of the world's woes.

Lerner summarizes well this "double helix" genetic ribbon of the faith: "Celebration of the grandeur of creation goes hand in hand with transformation of the social world".[6] To illustrate, he cites sabbath. Sabbath is both a day to give thanks for life and the blessing of creation and a day to remember liberation from slavery and our vocation of doxological witness to God as creator and redeemer.[7]

"God as creator and redeemer" invites theological and moral reflection on the contested relationship of creation and redemption in a theological ethic of life. Again, important clues are found in Hebrew scriptures.

Israel is redeemed from Egypt. Egypt is portrayed as the historical embodiment of the forces of chaos, that is, the powers of death, the anti-creational forces of the cosmos. And Israel is redeemed for a vocation — to embody redeemed creation as community. Israel is redeemed *for* life, even abundant life.

But there is no return to Eden or any normative Golden Age. Even the Promised Land, though rich with creation's bounty, is not pictured as the lost Garden of the Tree of Life. This is significant as implied commentary on the relation of redemption to creation, just as the choice to place Genesis before Exodus in the canon is significant. God's creative purpose for the whole universe (Genesis 1-11) is set out first in sacred scripture, and even the acknowledged "fulcrum text" of the election of Abraham (Genesis 12:1-3) immediately ties this election to "all the families of the earth".

Why no Eden, no Golden Age, no utopia, no portrayal of a fixed, normative created order? Why in fact are Adam and Eve themselves virtually absent from the rest of the Hebrew Bible? Is it because creation is not only not static, but not complete? The very commands of God in Genesis — to be fruitful and multiply (given to fish, birds and human earth creatures), to till and keep (to humans), to join in ongoing creation and joyful sabbath (extended to all creatures) — would seem to say that "good" here does not entail complete development or perfection. Divine creating is living, dynamic, continuing, unfinished. Old Testament scholar Terence Fretheim even says that "for the creation to stay just exactly as God originally created it would be a failure of the divine design". God's creating activity is not "exhausted in the first week of the world!"[8] All creation participates dynamically in it from one generation to the next.

Redemption serves creation. Redemption means reclaiming broken or despoiled or incomplete creation for life. It is not extra-creational or extra-human, much less extra-terrestrial! Redemption is Spirited actions, often very ordinary everyday ones, against the anti-creational forces that degrade and destroy. Yes, the ultimate goal is "a new heaven and a new earth". But even the most apocalyptic writings see this, like John of Patmos, as a radical transformation of the created order and not its utter obliteration in favor of realms literally out of this world.

Negatively, redemption means freeing Israel (and all creation) from all that oppresses or victimizes. Its reach is from inner spirit to socio-political and economic spheres to cosmic realms. Positively, redemption means realizing the life potential of all things.

Israel's own vocation is to become, in Fretheim's words, "a created co-reclaimer of God's intentions for the creation".[9] That vocation is as a "witness to the nations", however, and as such signals for all peoples their vocation as co-participants and "created co-reclaimers" of God's creating in the direction of and for the purposes of abundant life. Why does God redeem? For one reason only: because life and blessing are not yet gifts for all, or are precious gifts endangered.

We add that our own era has witnessed what we did not think possible: that human activities could overwhelm creation with chaos, life with death. We had not imagined, and do not yet comprehend, that we have in actual fact taken up a new vocation as co-*un*-creators, and on a scale that outstrips the potential of all previous generations.

To summarize: whatever else theology of life and ecumenical ethics might mean, they root here in the strong biblical sense of moral responsibility before the God who is the power in and of creation and the transcending power who beckons the redeeming transformation of creation in the steady direction of compassion and justice. From this God we receive the gift of life. Before and with this God, we are responsible for it.

But of course the theology of life does not end here. Indeed, neither does the Bible! The Bible's own moral trajectory remains incomplete, a matter of which the biblical communities were painfully aware and of which the prophets and Jesus constantly reminded them. The "good news" for some was sometimes bad news for others or no news at all. Good news for Abraham and Sarah was bad news for Hagar and Ishmael. Good news for freed slaves became bad news for peoples they took as slaves. The social patriarchy that runs throughout Scripture, even against its own theme of liberation and shared power, continues as bad news for women. Sexual ethics and Greek renditions of gender, nature, body, and mind in Hellenistic Judaism itself — and thus in formative Christian beginnings — continue as bad news for many to this day. Jewish biblical scholar Tikva Frymer-Kensky's conclusion is thus profoundly "biblical" when she says that "it is now our task to weave the rest of the Bible's religious faith..., in particular those [areas] that deal with the incorporation of all aspects of physicality, into our religious view of the universe".[10]

That is our task and more. The purpose of this opening section is only to say that while the biblical "moral project" of life clearly remains incomplete, an ecumenical theology and ethic of life should pursue it within the space marked by two interwoven themes: the healing, mending, and transforming of the world (tikkun olam) and the celebration of the gift of life itself as the gracious creation of a suffering and caring God in an awesome universe. The Bible's own theology of life turns on these themes.

THE CONTRIBUTION OF SCIENCE

The next contribution, offered by science, jumps from ancient sacred texts to recent discoveries.

A theology and ecumenical ethic of life poised at the cusp of a new millennium on an overburdened planet would do well to set before the eyes of faith the extraordinary unity we share with one another and all things, living and non-living. The unity is vividly supplied by two pictures science offers.

The first is the perspective presented by photographs of planet earth from space. The small blue, brown, green and white marbled planet, riding a tiny orbit in a vast universe, vividly says that we are all inhabitants of a single round space, occupants of one home, members of one finite, enclosed life-system. There may be life elsewhere in one of some 100,000,000,000 galaxies with billions and billions of stars each, but if so, we don't know of it. So far as we know, this fertile planet is the only Noah's Ark of life in the universe. Its thin envelope of life, then, is its distinctive feature.

The stirring image from space is more important as an image, even a religious image, than as an analysis. The latter is drawn from other satellite studies as well as innumerable ground-level ones. These show that for the first time in history human beings are slowly closing down the basic life systems of the planet and are actually changing their biophysical make-up in unprecedented, comparatively rapid and degrading ways. This includes the enveloping atmosphere itself. "The stark sign of our time is a planet in peril at our hands," says the blunt language of the WCC's Canberra assembly.[11]

The thirty years since the WCC's watershed world conference on Church and Society (Geneva, 1966), have accelerated what Hannah Arendt identified shortly before that meeting as the distinctive and highly problematic mark of the 20th century: we no longer "observe or take material from or imitate processes of nature [only] but seem actually to act into it". Furthermore, we seem "to have carried irreversibility and human unpredictability into the natural realm, where no remedy can be found to undo what has been done" or where undoing itself involves further destruction. This new capacity to act has a new level of consequences. Soon it not only begins "to overpower and destroy" humans themselves but also "the conditions under which life was given" to us.[12] This is the negative reality of occupying one space, one home, one round, finite, enclosed system, one saturated planet.

But whether viewed negatively or positively, *oikos* as "the household of life" is certainly the right word and symbol for our reality! Never has "oikoumene" been so important a notion or carried so rich a burden and message. "Ecumenical" does indeed mean the whole inhabited world — humankind and otherkind together in a precarious and undeniable unity of life and death. And "ecumenics" means realizing right relationship among the diverse members of the household so as to foster the flourishing of life for all. "Economics" means the "law" (*nomos*) of the household (*oikos*). It means arranging those societal systems which provide for the material well-being of all the planet's members and abiding by the rules of the ecosystems upon which each and every economic system is utterly dependent. "Ecology" is knowledge of the "house rules," or the "logic" (*logos*) of the oikos. It is knowledge of the interrelationship of organisms and their environment and of the mutual requirements for life together. On the grandest scale, it means living in accord with earth's basic requirements as a total biospherical system, including human society as the single most decisive element of that system. It means, in other words, acknowledging and respecting the integrity of creation and thus restraining human appetites in order to abide within nature's needs for its own regeneration and renewal. *Oikonomos* is usually translated "steward". But that is a weak way to signal broad human responsibility for the world we affect, a task entrusted us by no less than the creating, redeeming, sanctifying God.

For a life-centred ecumenical ethic, all this means just what Sallie McFague: "The moral issue of our day — and the vocation to which we are called — is whether we and other species will live and how well we will live."[13] Posed differently as a question: Is koinonia possible for the oikoumene on terms within hailing distance of shalom? Can koinonia encompass the fullness of life as the well-being of society and nature together?

The real and frightening unity of a common dynamic and destiny on a small planet is only one of the crucial reports offered by recent science. The other, potentially as important, is quite different at first glance. It is the common creation story now available from scientists and theologians alike.

We, and all else, are variations on exactly the same thing — stardust. The atoms in our bodies, and all atoms everywhere, were born in the supernova explosions of early stars. Everything is thus radically "kin" from the very beginning. When you look at the Southern Cross, Orion or the Big Dipper, the gnat on your arm, the flower near your path or the food on your plate, you are gazing at a neighbour who shares with you what is most basic of all — common matter together, as old and venerable as time and space themselves. In fact, if you look at more recent complex forms of life — plants and animals — you observe molecules which are very much the same. The most basic functions of cells are exactly the same in all life-forms. DNA and RNA processes and cell division processes are identical across life forms. (The DNA molecule specifies the characteristics of all living organisms, from bacteria through human beings.) "The wonderful lesson to come out of biology in the last five years," Victoria Foe explains, "is the same genes, the same parts, turn up again and again, from one species to another... The important lesson to realize is that we're all made of the same fabric, we're part of the same web."[14] The reason is remarkable: all life forms apparently share the same ancestor. We (all life forms) emerged from an ancient single-celled being.[15]

What could be a more radical and visible ecumenical unity than this! All that is (ta panta) has a common origin and is related in its most basic being.

Everything is also radically diverse and unique. Regrettably, we have poor eyesight and a cramped imagination, so we see and understand little of what surrounds us. Annie Dillard tells of biologists finding in one square foot of topsoil only one inch deep "an average of 1,356 living creatures... including 865 mites, 265 springtails, 22 millipedes, 19 adult beetles, and various numbers of 12 other forms..."[16] This does not include what may be up to two thousand million bacteria and millions of fungi, protozoa, algae and innumerable other creatures which make the topsoil the one inch of adamah it is![17]

Or, looking in another direction, we soon lose the capacity to take in what we can see or even imagine. We can take in a mountain or a portion of a forest or the horizon of a desert, the horse, the hut, the corn and the weather. But beyond that we can hardly even imagine our own galaxy, the Milky Way. This, our home port, is 100,000 light years in diameter and has somewhere between ten billion and one hundred billion stars (our census is crude). Nor can we quite imagine what fifteen billion years is (the age of the universe thus far).

The upshot is that the enduring unity that has been ours (humankind's and all else's) from the very beginning has evolved as highly complex networks characterized by staggering differentiation (how many varieties of mushrooms or coniferous trees are there?) and even implausible individuation (how many zebras have the same pattern of stripes?). Genetics itself teaches the uniqueness of the individual. Life — no, life and non-life, organic and inorganic matter together and continuous — is a radical unity marked by interrelated and interdependent fecundity and variety whose detail and wonder escapes our shriveled sight and imagination. When we do catch a glimpse, we are moved to psalms. But that is, alas, too rare a response. Most of the time we just assume that life is, and will go on.

The diversity and individuation we have described has its own expression within the human species. Our lives are concrete, particular and different. We are who we are in different places with different cultural, linguistic, religious, political, economic and gender traditions. We differ one from the next; no two among the five billion of us is a clone of the other. And if we could peer backwards or forwards a few thousand years, we might find it difficult even to recognize our genetic forebears and posterity as persons with whom we could share an afternoon's conversation about almost anything. Life, even life within the same "kind", is a many-splendoured thing.

This, then, is science's second contribution: the stunning portrayal of a common creation in which we are radically united with all things living and non-living, here and into endless reaches of space, and at the same time radically diverse and individuated, both by life-forms and within life-forms. And all of it is not only profoundly inter-related and inseparably interdependent but highly fine-tuned so as to evolve together. We are all — the living and not living, organic and inorganic — the outcome of the same primal explosion and same evolutionary history. All internally related from the very beginning, we are the varied forms of stardust in the hands of the creator God. This reality is the most basic text and context of life — and a theology of life.

One may hope that the sense of our home as this oikos in this *cosmos* will stimulate the same sense of creation's grandeur and eucharist (thanksgiving) to God for the gift of life which the biblical communities knew. But we should do even better, because this is in fact a description of immensity and intricacy which far surpasses anything known by the biblical communities. The weight of the nucleus of an atom of life (1,000,000,000,000,000,000,000,000 times less than a gram), the incomprehensible "genius" of DNA, the vastness of a cosmos we hardly have measures for — all this eluded even the most awestruck psalmist or the most imaginative prophet with their bold visions of creation redeemed. Little wonder that Thomas Berry calls the universe itself the primal expression of the divine and the primary revelational event. Little wonder he urges us all towards a mystique of the cosmos and the earth and says that "the universe, by definition, is a single gorgeous celebratory event".[18] Neither theology nor ethics has truly fathomed what science presents us as bearers of meaning and power and as cosmic story-tellers in an infinitely magnificent evolution, an evolution which is, however, gravely threatened by our presence, at least on the only oikos we know and the only one that is fine-tuned for our survival. We must pray aloud in deep humility before life's creator and sustainer and bow before all else (such as green plants) upon which we depend for every breath we take and every morsel that passes between our teeth.

Let us post a criterion in passing. Any "God-talk" in the necessarily particular theologies of life of different traditions and locales which has a notion of God that does not include the entire fifteen billion-year history of the cosmos and does not relate to all its entities, living and non-living, ancient forms and very recent ones (such as humans), speaks of a God too small.[19] Any theology of life which does not assert both radical unity and radical differentiation as reality and necessity together also fails.

Yet the universe as "a single gorgeous celebratory event" is not all that life says to us. There is also utter wretchedness and awful oppression. Indeed, it is not at all clear from either scientific evidence or common experience that life will triumph over death, at least in forms hospitable to us and numerous other of God's beloved creatures. In fact, it is the threats to life, rather than the celebration of it, that stimulated the ecumenical theology and culture of life initiative in the first place. So amidst deep and deepening gratitude for life, the turn is to healing and tending and transforming, with God, the fragile creation of which we are immensely privileged to be part. Anything less consigns millions to the most common and worst forms of hell we know. The contributions of science thus move with urgency into the concerns of life-centred ecumenical ethics and the quest for cultures of life.

LIFE-CENTRED ETHICS

In an essay on "Latin America and the Need for a Life-Liberating Theology", Ingemar Hedström writes:

In light of [the] ravaging of people and land in Central America, we realize that the preferential option for the poor, characteristic of Latin American liberation theology, must be articulated as a preferential option for life. To exercise this option is to defend and promote the fundamental right to life of all creatures on earth. The right to life in all its fullness involves partaking of the material base of creation, that is, of the material goods that permit life. All people, and not the powerful alone, must be availed of such goods; all people, not the powerful alone, must do so in a way that reserves rather than despoils the earth and other forms of life. In order to exercise this right in a just and sustainable way, we must rediscover our primal roots in the earth, as creatures of the earth.[20]

Ravaging of people and land. Hedström begins his essay with a citation from J. Combe and N. Geward: "All the great civilizations of the world began with the felling of the first tree... the majority of them disappeared with the felling of the last."

A life-centred ecumenical ethic begins with "the material base of creation, that is, of the material goods that permit life". The initial reason is confessional. Christianity, despite its checkered history under the influence of earth-denying and body-denying spiritualities, is radically a religion of incarnation. God is mediated in and through embodiment. God is sacramentally present as life in "the material goods that permit life". God is in, with and under the finite and creaturely. The second person of the Trinity is utter commitment to and testimony of the "physicality" of God in covenant with the earth, just as the first person expresses the unutterable mystery of God and the third person God's radical immanence and transcendence in the Spirit.[21] "The end of God's ways," Dietrich Bonhoeffer liked to quote from F.C. Oetinger, "is bodiliness."

The confessional statement is also a moral one. It means ethical priority for basic creaturely needs, lest "people and land" continue to be "ravaged" and God's good creation ever and again violated. We can discuss this dimension of a life ethic with commentary on two topics: community (koinonia) and power.

"We commit ourselves anew to living as a community which cares from creation," said the WCC Canberra assembly[22] But what does a caring community require?

For life, creatures need space. Without adequate hospitable habitat, we do not live. This is not only the case for humans, with our needs for food, water, shelter, work and festivity. All life-forms need particular space and habitat carefully fitted for them. This is the great element of "democracy" in life and its requisite equality: we all need a space for the basics of life itself.[23] Without that which good space provides — productive land, a hospitable atmosphere and healthy water, the numberless forms of life that provide for one another in intricate and astounding ecosystems — none of the other goods we cherish, including artistic and spiritual ones, is even possible. If justice means the fullest possible flourishing of creation under the conditions of various limits and constraints, then nothing is more basic to justice than adequate space for life's basics. It is the first requirement of community and thus the foundation of koinonia.

This leads Sallie McFague to the provocative remark that "geography... may well be the subject of the twenty-first century", since it raises questions like: Where is the best land and who has access to it? What good space is available on this planet and who controls it? Who cares for it? Who will inherit it and what will they receive?[24]

We do not inhabit abstract "space". We live in highly particular spaces and places, in particular and dynamic economic, social, ethnic, political, cultural and religious communities and hierarchies. So the question of "space" is specific, a matter of the tangled worlds we inhabit, worlds often in deep conflict over space and place. Issues of justice, peace and the integrity of creation come home as mundane issues within human populations as well as between human populations and other populations. Here, too, the ethical priority is basic creational needs. For this reason, "the ecological sin is the refusal of the haves to share space and land with the have nots."[25] Whether we name this *the* sin, as McFague does, or some other viable candidate, the point is much the same: no life-centred ethic can bypass either human requirements in their differences (what is needed for a particular people at a particular time for a viable habitat and way of life) or the requirements of non-human populations (what other species in their differences need for their own viable habitat). All discussions of koinonia should begin here.

One phenomenon of recent times is that viable community is breaking down almost everywhere, and we are amidst a long season of unavoidable and dangerous social experimentation in which the need is to preserve and build up sustainable local community while at the same time developing regional and global institutions of widespread participation. Churches have indispensable roles to play in this, both in the creation of koinonia within their own membership and in joining with movements of broader membership. This is the case whether the subject is an economics of sustainability, equity and solidarity, or reconciliation of groups at deep odds with one another and the mediation of conflict, or the slow upbuilding of civil society and basic moral formation for viable community.

A life-centred ecumenical ethic finally turns on the issue of power. It does so in many ways.

The first is the recognition, that the distinctive mark of our epoch is the quantum leap in human power to affect all of life in fundamental and unprecedented ways. Some of this is because of new capacities. Some stems from sheer cumulative effect (5 billion people going about their lives, rather than the 1.6 billion at the turn of this century). Some of it is the heavy and wildly disproportionate impact of certain populations (essentially the affluent nations and allied elites). But the outcome is that any ethic which does not track the effects of power in all relationships, intra-human and between human and otherkind, is blinded to the key moral reality of the age. Sustainable society and community cannot happen apart from power and its transformations.

There is another reason why a viable theological ethic of life turns on the matter of power. It lies at the heart of faith. It may come as a surprise to some, but Christians rarely talk about anything but power (despite their occasional reluctance about the word). Power claims are intrinsic to Christian ways of leaning into the world. The theme shakes itself loose in hymnody ("Holy, holy, holy, Lord God Almighty... Perfect in *power*, in love and purity"), in classic confessions ("We believe in God, the Father *Almighty*..."), in the most familiar prayer of all ("For thine is the kingdom, the *power* and the glory"), in preaching ("Our God is *able*..."), and in the first believers' convictions ("For the kingdom of God depends not on talk but on *power*" — 1 Corinthians 4:20). None of this should be a surprise, since the Scriptures themselves consistently portray God as power. God is the power to create, destroy, plant and pluck up, renew, redeem, restore, heal, save. Indeed, in the rituals and records of all peoples, divinity is itself associated with nothing so much as power. The *raison d'etre* of the sacred itself is nothing less than marking, evoking and channeling extraordinary power. For believers of many faiths, God is identified as the unsurpassed power who offers unsurpassed power for life. For basic reasons of faith, then, power belongs at the center of an ecumenical life ethic.[26]

There are other related reasons to insist on attention to power. Power is elemental to being itself. Power is what lets us and everything else, including all those creatures Annie Dillard's topsoil, to "stand out" from nothingness. Power is the flow of energy apart from which nothing that is, exists. Nothing good ever happens apart from power, just as nothing evil does, and for the very same reason: nothing happens apart from power. Nothing can.

This can and should be said theologically, in the way Orthodox Christians have for nearly two millennia: God is the uncreated energy of the created, energy-suffused universe. That means: God is a power-sharing God. That means: All power is from God. That means: power in its most elemental sense is simply "power to", the power of agency, human and non-human agency alike, in the vast web of this miracle we call life. And all of it, as the Orthodox also say, is the expression of God's own life. All of it, atom-to-atom, molecule-to-molecule, cell-to-cell, breath-to-breath, day in and day out. This is power at its most basic, power as cosmic energy and its flow, sometimes identified by religious peoples as the Spirit which animates all life. An adequate ethic asks what these elementary life-giving and life-sustaining flows mean for the way we live.

Two further dimensions of power belong to our discussion. The first is an analysis of the basic symbols, images, metaphors and models in our lives, and their internal connections to social arrangements and practices. This is true for all reigning symbols, images, and metaphors and models (in the media, in the marketplace, in our homes, in the public political sector). But I will illustrate with religious ones. We know from sociology and psychology of religion that we rather consistently image power "on earth as it is in heaven". That is, if you tell us your image of God (as opposed to your stated propositions about God) you will also tell us what is your image of power. Yet we too rarely do power analysis of critical, reigning Christian symbols. Instead, claims about the power of some symbol (the cross, for example) are substituted for analysis of the specific dynamic and outcome of that symbol's reality in and for the women and men and children in a given community and for our treatment of nature. Claims about the symbol are offered instead of a description of the way it actually functions as part of community power dynamics. We communicate images of God in various ways, but without telling how they are related to the social arrangements of power that shape the context, form and meaning of our lives together. Differently said, we don't ask how concrete material practices and social interactions are internally connected to our God-talk and our ethics-talk. Thus we are not enabled to see what powers are at work in our lives and how they are at work.

The analysis of symbols, images, metaphors and models leads to power analysis of the social arrangements themselves. This may take place along lines of race, gender, class, culture, ethnicity, sexual preference or almost any way in which human interaction is patterned. Are the power relationships in these patterns those of "power over", "power against", "power with and among", "power within", "power on behalf of", or what? Is the power at work reputational power, coalitional power, communicational power, structural power, charismatic power or some other form? It is overt or covert, masked or apparent? In short, what kind of power is operating by what dynamics and as constitutive of what kind of community relationships for what good or ill purposes?

Whatever particular theologies and ethics of life we articulate, then, the criteria should include viable habitat for all creatures, a place in nature and society which addresses basic creaturely needs and permits flourishing and power to pursue life's possibilities among ourselves in ways that aid and abet the same for others. Such criteria will mean church-advocated actions which are sometimes deconstructive (liberation from oppressive arrangements), sometimes reconstructive (creating more just and sustainable community arrangements) and sometimes prospective (sending signals of the kind of future which may not be possible in the present but is within the reach of hope).

All that remains is to reiterate Hedström's contention that a Christian life-centered ethic exercises "the preferential option for all life" and to spell out briefly its moral norms.

The option for all life may sound hopelessly "airy". But it is neither vague nor meaningless when understood in view of the passion and resurrection of Jesus at the heart of the Christian story. There it is revealed as quite specific: God's own way for the well-being of all creation means joining the suffering of creation, as a power there for life. Compassion (suffering with) is the passion of life itself, wherever suffering is a reality. It is the only way to life from the inside out. Power that does not go to the places where life, human and non-human alike, is most obviously ruptured, jeopardized or ruined is no power for healing at all. The only power that can heal and tend and transform creation is power drawn to the flawed and broken places, there by the grace and power of God to call forth powers the weak never knew they had, or to repudiate as destructive the powers of the strong who exploit. This is not suffering as itself a goal or good, both of which are serious pathologies. Nor is it a call to meritorious self-sacrifice. It is suffering in the manner of Jesus — joining God, through incarnational accompaniment of and involvement in creation's suffering, so as to turn us all towards life rather than death. In this manner the way of the cross is also the way of resurrection. When the church embodies this way as its own, it is the sign of new creation.

If this kind of compassion is the central disposition of a life-centred ethic for our time, the moral norms which serve the ethic are the following:

— *Sustainability*, as the ongoing capacity of natural and social systems to thrive together, both for current generations and future ones.

— *Participation*, as the inclusion of all involved voices in society's decisions, and in obtaining and enjoying the benefits of society as well as sharing its burdens.

— *Sufficiency*, as the commitment to meet the basic material needs of all life possible.

— *Solidarity*, as the obligation to stand with others, with a view especially to the most vulnerable of every community.

CONCLUSION

I do not believe a theology of life and ecumenical ethic is either desirable or possible except in the way Isasi-Diaz and Tarango say — articulated theological space inviting participation from lived life itself in all its variety. Dale Irwin is surely correct "that the ecumenical movement itself is, and always has been, a multi-faceted affair encompassing different historical and theological agendas which have never been reducible to one, and which resist being synthesized into a single coherent framework."[26] This is only a confirmation of what was said by the Second Vatican Council in its Decree on Ecumenism, *Unitatis Redintegratio*: "The heritage handed down by the apostles was received differently and in different forms, so that from the very beginnings of the church its development varied from region to region and also because of differing mentalities and ways of life" (para. 14). This does not mean that we cannot speak meaningfully of a conciliar movement or even of conciliar unity. It means that praxis in the ecumenical movement is always dynamic. It breaks old boundaries, reaches different crossroads, achieves new unities which bear new imperatives and discovers faith both as a steady guide and a permanent openness to God and the world.

It also means there will be no single theology of life or ecumenical ethic, cast in the form of a single consciousness with agreed-upon language and voice. It means that while we may achieve some common formulations, they themselves are best when they represent converging points of agreement that permit a diversity of local idioms and meanings. If there is one story we embrace, it is already in the manner of the four (different) gospels or in the manner of the earliest churches, scattered as they were on three continents around the Mediterranean and involving multiple cultures, languages, peoples and ways of life from the very onset of gospel proclamation.

What I have tried to do in this paper, then, is to create a meaningful space within which more particular theologies of life and life-centred ecumenical ethics might meaningfully be discussed. "A meaningful space" does not mean a "neutral" one or one without substantive judgments and interpretations. This paper has offered theological and ethical substance from biblical, scientific, theological and ethical sources which have ecumenical rootage and give some direction for discussion, and which in any case encourage rather than inhibit ecumenical voices and perspectives.

NOTES

[1]Ada Maria Isasi-Diaz and Yolanda Tarango, *Hispanic Women: Prophetic Voice in the Church*, San Francisco, Harper & Row, 1988, pp.2-3.

[2]Michael Lerner, "Jewish Liberation Theology", in Michael Zweig, ed., *Religion and Economic Justice*, Philadelphia, Temple University Press, 1991, p.131.

[3]Elaine Pagels, *Adam, Eve, and the Serpent*, New York, Random House, 1988.

[4]Cf. the title of Christopher Stone's recent book on environmental ethics, *The Gnat is Older than Man* (Princeton University Press, 1993), based on a passage from the Talmud: "The world was made for man, though he was the latecomer among its creatures. This was design. He was to find all things ready for him. God was the host who prepared dainty dishes, set the table, and then led his guest to his seat. At the same time man's late appearance on earth is to convey an admonition of humility. Let him beware of being proud, lest he invite the retort that the gnat is older than he."

[5]Lerner, *loc. cit.*, p.131.

[6]*Ibid.*

[7]*Ibid.*

[8]Terence Fretheim, "The Reclamation of Creation", *Interpretation*, XLV, 1991, p.358. I draw heavily from Fretheim for this discussion of the relation of creation and redemption.

[9]*Ibid.*, p.365.

[10]Tikva Frymer-Kensky, *In the Wake of the Goddesses: Women, Culture, and the Biblical Transformation of Pagan Myth*, New York, Free Press, 1992, p.220.

[11]"Giver of Life — Sustain Your Creation!", in *Signs of the Spirit*, official report of the WCC's seventh assembly, ed. Michael Kinnamon, Geneva, WCC Publications, 1991, p.55.

[12]Hannah Arendt, *The Human Condition*, Chicago, University of Chicago Press, 1958, p.238. The original context of Arendt's comments is a discussion of the role of forgiveness in human affairs, including political and policy affairs. She is saying that our actions on the biosphere are not as susceptible to "forgiveness" as are human's actions upon one another. The consequences are not as easily "forgiven", courses are not as easily altered, nor new beginnings with a different set of consequences undertaken.

[13]Sallie McFague, *The Body of God: An Ecological Theology*, Minneapolis, Fortress, 1993, p.9.

[14]"Drawing Big Lessons From Fly Embryology", *The New York Times*, August 10, 1993, p.C12.

[15]Cf. Charles Birch and John Cobb, *The Liberation of Life: From the Cell to the Community*, Denton, Texas, Environmental Ethics Books, 1990, p.45: "The evolution of a living cell from organic molecules may have happened more than once on the earth. But probably only one original cell gave rise to all the rest of life on earth. This seems to be the only possible explanation of the basic similarity of the cells of all living organisms... Life is like a great branching tree with one central stem."

[16]Annie Dillard, *Pilgrim at Tinker Creek: A Mystical Excursion into the Natural World*, New York, Bantam, 1974, p.96, cited by McFague, op. cit., p.38.

[17]McFague, p. 9

[18]Thomas Berry, *The Dream of the Earth*, San Francisco, Sierra Club Books, 1988, p.5.

[19]This is Sallie McFague's effort to "sober" what she calls "our natural anthropocentrism"; *op. cit.*, p.104.

[20]Ingemar Hedström, "Latin America and the Need for a Life-Liberating Theology", in *Liberating Life: Contemporary Approaches to Ecological Theology*, ed. Charles Birch et al., Maryknoll, NY, Orbis, 1990, p.120.

[21]These are the suggestive terms of McFague, op. cit., pp.161f. Paul Tillich argued that Spirit itself is the most adequate way to speak of God in our time. Spirit unites power (Tillich's way of speaking of the depths of the divine) with *meaning* (the Logos) in such a way that they mean "life" or the "spirit." "The statement that God is Spirit means that life as spirit is the inclusive symbol for the divine life", cf. *Systematic Theology*, Chicago, University of Chicago Press, 1951, I, p.250, and the whole of Vol. III on the Holy Spirit. The WCC has, leading up to and after the Canberra assembly, given focus to the Spirit, but I suspect we have only begun to understand it as the meeting place for all our discussion and work, including with people of other faiths.

[22]Kinnamon, ed., *op. cit.*, p.55.

[23]James Nash and others argue correctly that the moral and legal notion of "rights" must be extended from "human rights" to the even more inclusive notion of "biotic rights". See Nash, *Loving Nature: Ecological Integrity and Christian Responsibility*, Nashville, Abingdon, 1991, esp. pp.162-91; and "Human Rights and the Environment: New Challenge for Ethics", in *Theology and Public Policy*, Vol. IV, no. 2, Fall 1992, pp.42-57.

[24]McFague, *op. cit.*, p.101.

[25]McFague, *ibid.*, p.117.

[26]Cf. Larry L. Rasmussen, "Power Analysis: A Neglected Agenda in Christian Ethics", in *The Annual of the Society of Christian Ethics,* Washington, Georgetown University Press, 1991.

[26]Dale Irwin, "Hearing Many Voices: Dialogue and Diversity in the Ecumenical Movement", doctrinal dissertation, Union Theological Seminary, New York, 1988, pp.4-5.

Appendix IIIh.

WCC delegation to the Kyoto Summit on Climate Change, "Statement to the High Level Segment of the Third Session of the Conference of the Parties (COP3) to the UN Framework Convention on Climate Change", Kyoto, Japan, December 9, 1997.

Mr. President, Distinguished Delegates, Observers,

We recognize that the COP3 negotiations are at a difficult point. We make this statement on behalf of the World Council of Churches with a combination of humility and prayer, wanting to assist the process and yet needing to speak the truth as we discern it.

For us in the World Council of Churches, the core of the COP3 agenda is <u>justice</u>.

Justice means being held responsible for one's actions.
> The rich of the world, through promotion of the current economic model, have been and continue to be responsible for the vast majority of emissions causing human-produced climate change but seem unwilling to honestly acknowledge that responsibility and translate it into action. It is ironic that countries which exult in their domestic legal principles feel themselves above the law when it comes to their international obligations on climate change.

Justice means being held accountable for promises you make.
> The rich of the world have broken their Rio promise to stabilise emissions by 2000 at 1990 levels and yet seem to exhibit no embarrassment at their failure.

Justice means being held responsible for the suffering you cause to others.
> Small island states, millions of environmental refugees, and future generations will suffer as a result of the callous exploitation of the Earth's resources by the rich.

Justice means being held accountable for abuse of power.
> Human societies, particularly in the over-developed countries, are damaging the environment through climate change with little respect for the inherent worth of other species which we believe to be loved by God as are we.

Justice means an equitable sharing of the Earth's resources.

> Millions of people lack the necessities for a decent quality of life. It is the height of arrogance to propose that restrictive commitments be placed on the poor to make up for the delinquencies of the rich. Over-consumption of the rich and poverty of the poor must both be eliminated to ensure quality of life for all.

Justice demands truth.

> Destructive misinformation campaigns are being used by groups with powerful economic self-interest with the intention of preventing meaningful action on climate change.

Justice requires honesty.

> The world is not so easily divided into the rich North and the poor South as we used to think. There are a few wealthy and powerful countries and elites within the category referred to as developing countries who sometimes misuse this classification of nations to disguise their economic self-interest.

God's justice is strict but it is not cruel. We are all here in Kyoto as brothers and sisters equal before God within the community of creation - a creation which we all want to be healthy and thriving for future generations. In affirmation of the goodness of creation (Genesis1:25), God beckons us to respect all forms of life. In what we do at COP3, we must not betray life.

Confidence-building measures are needed so that together we can reduce the threat of climate change:

- Industrialised countries must demonstrate, in the near future, real and significant reductions in domestic greenhouse gas emissions which many studies have shown to be possible with a considerable net benefit to their economies.

- Though developing countries should not be subject to formal emission limitation commitments yet, many of them are pursuing measures and can continue their efforts to become more energy-efficient and to limit greenhouse gas emissions.

- The sharing of finance and technological resources is needed but it is also very important to exchange experiences from both South and North including those of indigenous cultures, women's organisations and others which can offer lessons and tools for learning to live in a socially just, equitable and ecologically sustainable manner.

In these remaining days of COP3, let us shift our energies away from trying to figure out how to attain the minimum and channel them instead toward creative risk-taking options for accomplishing the maximum. Thank you.

Notes

[1] At COP3, the World Council of Churches (WCC) has been represented by a delegation consisting of:

Lic. Elías Crisóstomo Abramides, Ecumenical Patriarchate, Argentina

Ms. Nafisa Goga D'Souza, India

Dr. David G. Hallman, Canada (Head of Delegation)

Mr. Prawate Khid-Arn, Christian Conference of Asia, Hong Kong

Dr. Karin Léxen, Christian Council of Sweden, Sweden

Dr. Alfredo Salibián, Consejo Latinoamericano de Iglesias, Argentina

Rev. Tsutom Shoji, National Council of Churches in Japan, Japan

Rev. Bill Somplatsky-Jarman, National Council of Churches of Christ, United States of America

Dr. Larisa Skuratovskaya, Russia

[2] The World Council of Churches (WCC) has been involved in the climate change issue for ten years. To encourage governments of industrialised countries to accept their responsibility in the lead-up to COP3, the WCC co-ordinated a petition campaign through the churches in 23 industrialised countries which called on those governments to meet the stabilisation commitment of Rio, adopt a binding international agreement for further reductions post-2000, and engage citizen participation more forcefully in finding solutions.

[3] The "Kyoto Appeal" presented at the Dec. 7th Inter-Religious Gathering on Climate Change (including Buddhists, Christians, Shintos and New Religions) contains prayers for COP3 and calls on leaders to support the AOSIS protocol. Copies are available from members of the WCC delegation.

Appendix IIIi.

WCC Delegation to the Fifth Session of the UN Commission on Sustainable Development, "Building a Just and Moral Economy for Sustainable Communities"; April 10, 1997, New York.

Mr. Chairman and Distinguished Delegates,

We appreciate the opportunity to address you in the name of the Commission of the Churches on International Affairs of the World Council of Churches. The Council represents 325 Orthodox, Protestant and Anglican churches in over 130 countries around the world with a combined membership of about 400 million people.

This 5th Session of the CSD is intended to review progress toward sustainable development since the 1992 Earth Summit in Rio de Janeiro in preparation for the UN General Assembly Special Session in June. We fear that the assessment will be inadequate because important questions are not being asked.

In our own work, we are regularly questioning the term "sustainable development". We find it often misused in order to legitimize current economic approaches which are premised on unlimited economic growth and a continuous and unregulated expansion of production and consumption for the world's rich. Thus to measure progress toward sustainable development in this context is to avoid challenging the very dynamics which are increasing the gap between the rich and the poor in the world and causing environmental destruction. We call upon governments, international institutions and people of good will to demonstrate moral courage and political will to confront the excesses of globalization.

The Council understands that all economic systems must be tested from the perspective of their effect on the poor, the oppressed and the marginalized. God has created the whole cosmos to be good; it is a common inheritance for all peoples for all times to be enjoyed in just, loving and responsible relationships with one another. This understanding is foundational in our vision of a just and moral economy where: a) people are empowered to fully participate in making decisions that affect their lives, b) public and private institutions and enterprises are accountable and held responsible for the social and environmental impacts and consequences of their operations, and c) the earth and whole created order is nurtured with utmost respect and reverence rather than exploited and degraded.

Our vision of a just and moral economy places on us the responsibility to build and nurture economies that put people and the environment first.

We speak increasingly of "sustainable community" because it implies the nurturing of equitable relationships both within the human family and also between humans and the rest of the ecological community - in other words, justice within the whole of God's creation.

The question we should be asking at this CSD and the Special Session is "what must we do to bring about justice and attain sustainable community?"

Within the human family, many people lack health, security, hope. The member churches of the WCC around the world are intensely involved in the everyday struggles of people for sustainable community. Thus, our understandings emerge from our real-life experience. Let us share three examples.

Our first example concerns women in Sri Lanka. Structural Adjustment Policy dictated the replacement of hill country forest land with export tobacco cultivation. The trees helped retain the moisture which was the source for mountain streams; now they were gone and the water flow was significantly reduced. This forced the women tea workers of the area to climb extra distances to fetch their daily water. In addition to increasing the workload of these women, insufficient water has added to the health hazards of the entire community. Going beyond their traditional roles, the women, along with children, organized themselves to plant trees on those hills where soil erosion was most evident with the hope that tomorrow these hills will once again be covered with streams.

For Indigenous Peoples, sustainable development is integrally linked to their struggle for recognition of rights to self determination, control over ancestral lands, resources and indigenous knowledge systems. Traditional practices for sustainable production and consumption are under threat from the negative impacts of globalization and trade liberalization. This new face of colonization, perpetuated by the often aggressive policies of governments and TNCs, has seen extensive extraction of resources from Indigenous Peoples lands in deforestation, mining and dam building. Also, Indigenous Peoples are confronted with the increase in bioprospecting and genetic engineering, practices that pose a direct threat to the protection of their intellectual cultural property rights. Thus Indigenous Peoples are continually challenging governments and international institutions to establish meaningful participatory mechanisms in the preservation of sustainable community.

Our churches are actively addressing the issue of climate change. We see it as an ethical issue. Because of the economies and consumption-oriented lifestyles of the industrialized nations, the consequences of climate change will be suffered disproportionately by the poorer developing nations, low-lying states, and future generations. It is not just the human family that will be adversely affected by climate change but all the ecosystems of the planet. The peoples and ecosystems of the Pacific Islands are among the most vulnerable to the impacts of climate change through rising sea levels and tropical storms.

Humanity is threatened. The earth is threatened. We see some common sources of this threat. In an address to the Copenhagen World Social Summit, WCC General Secretary Konrad Raiser said:

> "As the world economy becomes global in nature, economic and political power is increasingly concentrated in the hands of the privileged few. The global market approach is rapidly reshaping the world, weakening the traditional role of national governments through policies of deregulation and limiting the effectiveness of the system of intergovernmental social institutions. Who is to look after the people's interests in a time when institutions in the private sphere assume an ever greater role in the shape of the global economy? Who is to safeguard the rights of the poor nations and the small states in the face of the domination of a handful of powerful actors on the world scene?"

A current example which is of great concern to us is the emerging power of the World Trade Organization whose decisions will supercede the authority of national governments and/or international institutions, including the CSD. We question the idolatry which is often bestowed upon the notions of free trade, market access, speculative investment, and competition, seemingly at any cost. The process for making decisions in the WTO and related bodies is highly secretive, non-participatory, and dominated by the interests of transnational corporations. It is not just civil society that is excluded from the table but even many parts of national governments are kept in the dark. This exclusion is most severe for the governments and civil societies in countries of the economic South.

If we are to work toward sustainable community for all, then local, national and global priorities must be based on justice, peace and respect for the integrity of creation.

The World Council of Churches recommends that:

1. National, regional and international policies and programmes in economic, social and environmental areas should be based on criteria of sustainable community with specific principles, indicators and assessment procedures to measure progress. In this context, we endorse the proposal of regular Rio review processes to assess progress and roadblocks for sustainable development e.g. Earth Summit III in 2002.

2. WTO proceedings and decision-making should be transparent and inclusive allowing full participation of all countries and meaningful access for representatives of civil society such as non-governmental organizations. The WTO should be formally accountable within the UN system.

3. In reference to women, we need to implement the Beijing agreement and go beyond to create new development strategies that would promote both sustainable livelihoods and communities, based on gender and social equity for all sectors of society.

4. The CSD promote:
—the immediate adoption of the UN Draft Declaration on the Rights of Indigenous Peoples which provides minimum standards for the continued existence of Indigenous communities; the establishment of a Permanent Forum in the UN for Indigenous Peoples; facilitate greater participation of Indigenous Peoples in the CSD sessions and the related processes.

5. In terms of climate change, governments of industrialized countries should a) fulfil their promise at the Rio Earth Summit to stabilize CO_2 emissions by the year 2000 at 1990 levels, b) establish firm policy measures and agree to a binding international agreement which will achieve greater reductions after 2000, and c) engage public discussion on the risks of climate change and increase public participation in finding solutions.

6. The CSD should recommend that a high-level segment of the Economic and Social Council be devoted to the theme of globalization and sustainability.

We pledge to work with peoples of all faiths to pursue these goals.

Appendix IIIj.

Mercy Oduyoye, "The Meaning and the Signs of Solidarity", *Who will Roll the Stone Away?: The Ecumenical Decade of the Churches in Solidarity with Women,* **Geneva: WCC, 1990, pp.43-49.**

There are several words whose meanings we can only understand through personal experience. Solidarity is one such. I remember the time in my own life when I came to use the word solidarity from my innermost being. Solidarity is when people you did not even know existed or, if you did, you never expected to be involved in your affairs as persons, see you and say to you: "We prayed for you; we took courage from your stand." Or they contact you with messages of encouragement and prayer.

Solidarity became for me the antithesis of operating from a basis of conflict and contest. Solidarity at that time meant sympathy and various degrees of empathy. For me, it was people exhibiting ties of affection derived from a feeling of being on the same wavelength with me. Somehow these persons had entered into what I was going through and felt they shared the world-view and ideas that were prompting my decisions and determining my actions. They understood my struggle and identified themselves with me. I am sure that some of these people are still unknown to me, and some only know me by name; but I feel their presence and influence in my life very vividly. That, for me, was solidarity.

Am I in solidarity with these people? This brings us to another aspect of the word's meaning. People who support good causes do so for a variety of reasons, not all of which have to do with the persons whose lives are linked with the issues or the causes. Solidarity with a human face is mutual and reciprocal. It involves elements of cooperation, rapport and sharing. It develops between and among people who are bonded in harmony. Solidarity is walking hand in hand, developing strength through unity so that common interests are protected and common aims are achieved.

To ask the entire church to be in solidarity with women is to ask for identification with the hopes and fears women live by and with, in church and society. The Decade call assumes there is an undivided church, and asks the church to care for the totality of its membership. It is a call for inclusiveness in all aspects of church life. It asks the church to live and witness in such a way as to demonstrate that its interests are those of the whole community. If the interests of any sector are overlooked the church ceases to function as one community. It becomes less than the church of Christ in which love and mutual support must be the order.

If the Decade is perceived as liable to give rise to conflict, so be it. For to register dissent over what does not make for bonds of harmony and peace is a Christian duty. Conflict is necessary, for when the common good is conceived as that which benefits only a part of the community there is no health in the body. The differences have to be acknowledged and dealt with. A resolution must be attempted so that within the body of Christ we do not work at cross purposes. If we do, it becomes "a house divided against itself". Therefore it is a sign of life to recognize the pain in the body which has led to the call for the Decade. The church is asked to be in solidarity with women because in the body of Christ the women members are in pain (as are some men) because we seem to be operating as if we are unsure whether women are fully human and therefore to be accounted responsible and accountable.

In some countries the hurt is dealt with by women escaping from the scene of their dehumanization. There are tensions and contentions in many congregations and church institutions. Discussions are polarized on gender lines. Many women are alienated from the institutional church, and many men and women are irritated by the stance of women who dare to voice different opinions. Some women are being treated as scapegoats; they are accused of "stirring up trouble" in churches. Simply because they have a different perception of their role in church and society.

Within the membership of the WCC, solidarity with women is a tenuous factor. Recommendations painfully and painstakingly made on this issue seem to apply only to the churches-in-council and not to the individual member churches. Solidarity with women means different things for different churches. That is why the Decade efforts take different forms. Sometimes one is inclined to wonder whether the churches are in solidarity with the Council on this issue. Agreements on principles do not match the practices of several member churches and often one is inclined to conclude that the Council and its members are not of one mind. Through the Decade the WCC is encouraging the churches to listen more carefully to women, and to review attitudes that prevent women from feeling at home in the church. Solidarity with women means examining why women sometimes want to establish parallel structures.

BIBLICAL SOLIDARITY

Events in the history of the Hebrew people as they are recorded in the Bible, and the experiences of the early church as it began to spread, give us examples of what we may describe as biblical solidarity- and also its opposite, life-denying acts simply called sin. Of course solidarity is not always in support of life-affirming purposes. Sometimes it does not work in conformity with the purposes of God; it is not in solidarity with God, if we may put it so boldly. Adam and Eve agreed together on the supreme act of disobedience, daring God. Coming together to build the Tower of Babel is a striking example of solidarity. So is the family of Noah in the Ark. But while the former was undertaken for the glory of a people who wanted to make a name for themselves, the latter was solidarity anchored on the will of God. Biblical stories about the beginnings of life, like such stories in African traditions, are realistic about competing powers of life and death.

The call for solidarity with women is a call to life according to God's will. Biblical solidarity is reviewed from this life-enhancing perspective.

Joseph, who became the governor of all of Egypt, had brothers who were not brotherly in their feelings towards him. They had even sold him into slavery. But God used their failure in love for the preservation of the children of Israel from the great famine. Joseph met the needs of his people, a people who had no use for him but who were the people whom God had given him as his kin. Like Moses in later history, he identified with a people in trouble when he could have stayed away and disowned all relationship. As a prince in Egypt there was no need for Moses to identify with the suffering of the whole tribe; they did not even ask for it. Moses was a reluctant collaborator with God but a collaborator all the same. The vision of a promised land with a people under God's rule kept him at his task to the end. Biblical solidarity happens when people act with God to end oppression and to build new communities of freedom in partnership with God.

In the Moses story we recall the solidarity of women with women. The Egyptian midwives and the Hebrew mothers came together. An Egyptian princess and slave girls co-operated to save the life of a baby boy, who was to be God's agent for the liberation of Israel. To put an end to brutality and to rescue persons from dehumanization, God does not only perform miracles that clearly interfere with the order of nature. In the Bible more often God inspires and empowers human beings to take on the challenge.

I have often wondered how Moses felt when he came to admit to himself what must have been an open secret among the women who brought him up to manhood. Solidarity with people demands acceptance of our common humanity, our common origins as children of the one God.

A church acting in solidarity with women will be living out the Christian theology of creation and the Christian anthropology that see humanity - male and female - as bearers of the image of the one God.

Biblical solidarity may sometimes appear like an act of treason. Rahab, the woman who hid the would-be invaders of her own city and gave them shelter, cannot be considered a good citizen. She was breaking ranks, and making the city vulnerable. But bonds of friendship empower one to protect life even against one's own heritage and interests.

Friendship such as we find between David and Jonathan, Ruth and Naomi, Elijah and Elisha, is captured in the words: "As the Lord lives, your life upon it, I will not leave you." Take the case of the rape of Tamar by Amnon; "patriarchal justice" would have contrived to have her stoned as a prostitute. Her brother Absalom took her side against such injustice (2 Sm.13). Many contemporary men have failed this test, for they do not find it easy to listen to women, let alone take them seriously. For some men solidarity with women often seems like letting the side down.

What the Decade call says is that in solidarity the only side is that of truth and justice. It demands seeing the church as one whole and humanity as a single unit in God's creation. Solidarity demands standing for the truth even at the cost of being a lone voice, standing like a Daniel for a Susanna against the guiles of corrupt judges and false witnesses.

Biblical solidarity means leading the sick to the source of healing, like the slave-girl who advised Naaman. She participated in the healing of Naaman by providing the right information (Kings 6:1-19). Sharing information in this case was enough to being the process of change; but in the case of the man suffering from paralysis in the Gospel of Mark, providing information was not enough; those who cared for the man had to carry him bodily to the healer.

In many cases solidarity calls for lending a hand, making provision for the needy. Solidarity demands acting as the widow of Zarephath did to the prophet Elijah (1

Kings 17:1-24); or like the hospitable woman in Shunem who looked after Elisha (2 Kings 4:8-37). Solidarity may demand of some to "let go", and to be a Cyrus to the hopes of an Ezra. When Cyrus, King of Persia, heard the call of the "Lord God of Heaven" to build for him a house in Jerusalem, he encouraged the Jews to go back to Jerusalem, and their neighbours assisted them with gifts of every kind (Ezra 1:5-11). Unlike in Babel, they were building for the glory of God, and they experienced the solidarity even of the strangers among whom they lived as exiles.

The empowerment of Nehemiah by King Artaxerxes included not only permission to leave but letters of introduction to the governors of the territories through which he journeyed. Often that is all it takes to demonstrate solidarity: enable people to pass through difficult territory.

Solidarity is not only verbal and ideological, it has to be expressed in concrete liberative acts. Solidarity is more than letting go. Freed slaves, who have no resources other than being physically alive, have a hard time being free. "Wherever each man lives, let his neighbours help him with god… and votive offerings for the Lord's temple in Jerusalem." This is from the edict of Cyrus, King of Persia, permitting all under him who were of Jewish origin to return and rebuild the temple. Twice David was called to account for taking the side of the poor in word, while his acts spoke the language of exploitation and theft (2 Sam. 11-12:14; 14:1-24). It is no wonder, then, that those who are called to be in solidarity often resist the call. "I have never been a man of ready speech," said Moses. The solidarity road is not a smooth one, and it can be traversed only if we keep before us the ultimate aim, that of a Canaan, a land where God is the ruler of the people.

Jesus has handed over the care of humankind to the church, certainly the care of those who name his name. If the church fails, it will hear the words of Ezekiel:

> Should not the shepherd care for the sheep? You consume the milk, wear the wool, and slaughter the fat beasts, but you do not feed the sheep. You have not encouraged the weary, tended the sick, bandaged the hurt, recovered the straggler, or searched for the lost; and even the strong you have driven with ruthless severity. (Ezek. 34:34).

Appendix IIIk.

"Together on the Way, Resisting Domination – Affirming Life: the Challenge of Globalization", Eighth Assembly, Harare, Report of the Policy Reference Committee II, 1999. "Together on the Way, 5.3. Globalization", Eighth Assembly, Harare, 1999

"Together on the Way, Resisting Domination – Affirming Life: the Challenge of Globalization", Eighth Assembly, Harare, Report of the Policy Reference Committee II, 1999.

Globalization is a reality of the world today - an inescapable fact of life. All people are affected. Globalization is not simply an economic issue. It is a cultural, political, ethical and ecological issue. Increasingly, Christians and churches find themselves confronted by the new and deeply challenging aspects of globalization which vast numbers of people face, especially the poor. The vision behind globalization is a competing vision of the oikoumene, the unity of humankind and the whole inhabited earth. How do we live our faith in the context of globalization?

Gathered in Harare

1. Gathered in Harare, this eighth assembly of the World Council of Churches, has listened to the voices of the people of Africa during the Africa plenary and padare. Those voices included both cries of pain and suffering, but also testimonies of resistance, faith and hope. The remarkable strength, creativity and spiritual vitality of our African sisters and brothers is an inspiration to us all. Together we were reminded of the vision of a free people which inspired Africa's struggle for liberation from colonialism.

2. That vision is still alive in the struggles of the people for daily livelihood, to sustain their community life, to be nourished by the rich traditions and values inherited from the past, to live in harmony with the earth, to find space to express themselves. People are longing to live in dignity in just and sustainable communities. We resonated to their vision and aspirations because, though we come from all parts of the world, experience the same yearnings.

3. In the midst of these visions for our people, and our children's children, we have become more acutely aware that, in some fundamental respects, the legacy of colonialism of the past is still present with us in a new form — a form perhaps more

seductive on the surface, but demeaning and dangerous at deeper levels. The driving forces of this new form of domination are economic powers which may be as insidious as political colonizers and a subtle but powerful ideology which assumes that the most promising way to improve the quality of life for all people is to give free rein to market forces.

Concentration of power

4. Today, despite the independence of many formerly colonized peoples, power is increasingly concentrated in the hands of a relatively few nations and corporations particularly in the North. Their power extends across the globe and into many areas of life. Their power is extensive and intensive. Major decisions are made by these 30 or so nations and 60 giant corporations. The intentional globalization of production, capital and trade further strengthens the power of the financial centers of the global market.

5. Globalization affects all of us. It contributes to the erosion of the nation state, undermines social cohesion, and intensifies the conquest of nature in a merciless attack on the integrity of creation. Debt crisis and Structural Adjustment Programmes became instruments to gain more control over national budgets and create a profitable and safe environment for investments by the private sector at unbearable costs for the people.

6. This process is greatly strengthened by the development of global communications and media networks. It is also accompanied by a very costly, but successful strategy by the USA and other developed countries to gain and secure military and political hegemony on a global scale. The forging of new institutions, like the World Trade Organization and the proposed Multilateral Agreement on Investment, solidify the power of the already privileged. The convergence of such factors in the 1990s represents a new level of challenge to the poor, the vast majority of the world's population.

7. The concomitant homogenization in the process of globalization does not include labour. While the movement of global capital is unrestricted, new barriers are created to keep migrant workers in check. In the face of globalization labour is controlled and is losing its strength. Although the liberalization of trade is high on the agenda of economic globalization, developed countries still protect their local agriculture and certain industries against the import of competitive products. They still subsidize their exports with often devastating effects for local markets in the South.

Poverty and exclusion

8. We recognize that there are potentially positive aspects of this burgeoning globalization. As we have seen, new technologies often have linked people against current injustices and abuses of power. They can be used to alert the Christian community of persecutions, violation of human rights, human needs, and emergencies. Easier and efficient accessibility across regions facilitates solidarity among social movements and networks.

9. Those who defend the free market argue that free market economies have demonstrated remarkable capacity to produce goods and services in a world which has a desperate need to meet people's basic material needs. While they acknowledge that some economies have been distorted by being more closely linked to the world economy, they also emphasize that sometimes this link has afforded new levels of prosperity. Such alleged benefits of globalization make it attractive to those who see an unfettered free market system as a way out of poverty.

10. The reality of unequal distribution of power and wealth, of poverty and exclusion, however, challenges the cheap language of a global shared community. The often-used image of the "global village" is misleading. The new situation is lacking exactly the sense of community, belonging and mutual accountability that is typical of village life. Global media networks promote a consumerist monoculture. The situation of many poor people deteriorates. The World Bank has concluded recently that in 1998 the number of countries with negative economic growth had grown from 21 to 36 during the past year. As a result, they observed that fiscal policies and interest rates have had a much greater social cost than originally envisaged.

11. Further, only a small fraction of the one and one-half trillion dollars of currency exchange each day is related to basic economic activities. The great proportion is mere financial speculation, not genuine investment. That speculation weakens further the already weak economies. Massive speculation led to the collapse of financial markets in Asia and risks to jeopardize the global economy as a whole.

12. The life of the people is made more vulnerable and insecure than ever before. Exclusion in all its forms breeds violence that spreads like a disease. The number of migrants desperately searching for jobs and shelter for their families is increas-

ing dramatically. In the industrialized countries of Europe and North America pockets of the poor are growing in number and size. Everywhere, the gap between rich and poor is widening, making Indigenous Peoples, women, youth and children the primary victims of poverty and exclusion. The vast majority of those excluded are inevitably people of colour who are targets of xenophobia, racism and oppression.

Contradictions, tensions and anxieties

13. Globalization gives rise to a web of contradictions, tensions and anxieties. The systemic interlocking of the local and the global in the process created a number of new dynamics. It led to the concentration of power, knowledge, and wealth in institutions controlled or at least influenced by transnational corporations. But it also generated a decentralizing dynamic as people and communities struggle to regain control over the forces that threaten their very existence. In the midst of changes and severe pressure on their livelihoods and cultures, people want to affirm their cultural and religious identities. While globalization universalized certain aspects of modern social life, it also causes and fuels fragmentation of the social fabric of societies. As the process goes on and people lose hope, they start to compete against each other in order to secure some benefits from the global economy. In some cases this reality gives rise to fundamentalism and ethnic cleansing.

Neo-liberal ideology

14. Economic globalization is guided by the neo-liberal ideology. The credo of the free market is the firm belief that through competing economic forces and purposes, an 'invisible hand' will assure the optimum good as every individual pursues his or her economic gain. It views human beings as individuals rather than as persons in community, as essentially competitive rather than cooperative, as consumerist and materialist rather than spiritual. Thus, it produced a graceless system that renders people surplus and abandons them if they cannot compete with the powerful few in global economy.

15. As a consequence, people tend to lose their cultural identity and deny their political and ethical responsibility. Promising wealth for everybody and the fulfilment of the dream of unlimited progress, neo-liberalism draws a picture of universal salvation. But obsessed with rising revenues from financial markets, expansion of trade and growth of production, the global economic system is blind for its destructive social and ecological consequences.

A challenge to the churches and the ecumenical movement

16. Globalization poses a pastoral, ethical, theological and spiritual challenge to the churches and the ecumenical movement in particular. The vision behind globalization is a competing vision of the oikoumene, the unity of humankind and the whole inhabited earth. The globalized oikoumene of domination is in contrast with the oikoumene of faith and solidarity that motivates and energizes the ecumenical movement. The logic of globalization needs to be challenged by an alternative way of life of community in diversity.

17. Plurality and diversity within the ecumenical movement, for example, are no longer seen as an obstacle to the unity of the churches and a viable future for humankind. Diversity provides rich resources and options for viable solutions if the stories, experiences and traditions of others are recognized and individual Christians, ecumenical groups and churches search together for alternatives that affirm and sustain life on earth. The traditional concept of the catholicity of the church deserves renewed attention. The notion and praxis of catholicity can be understood as an early form of Christian response to the imperial form of unity that was shaped and represented by the Roman Empire. Such an alternative option to the imperial power is of relevance for the affirmation of the ecumenical dimension in the life of the churches in the context of globalization.

Jubilee and globalization

18. During these days together we have been reminded often of the jubilee, a time of emancipation, restoration of just relationships and new beginnings (Lev. 25, Isa. 61, Luke 4). The jubilee is a recognition that, left to its normal and uninterrupted course, power becomes more and more concentrated in a few hands, that without intervention every society slides into injustice. As the Hebrew Bible reminds us, the powerful build house upon house, appropriate field after field (Isa. 5:8). The weak and poor are vulnerable, marginalized, excluded. Restoration requires to turn against this course of history (Mic. 7; Neh. 5). The wholeness of people, and of a people, requires the intervention, the periodic breaking down of the ordinary course of events.

19. The jubilee has important implications for our reflections on globalization today. Globalization usually appears benign, or even beneficial, especially when one benefits from that process. But the increasing concentration of power — economic, political, cultural, military — is dramatically shaping the world of the present and future in ways that are not benign. The scandal of crippling debt, the

marginalization and exclusion of vast numbers of sisters and brothers, the exploitation of women and children, additional strain on minorities struggling to keep their culture, religious tradition and language alive, the destruction of the ancestral land of Indigenous Peoples and their communities are in part an expression of this concentration of power legitimized in the name of a better standard of living.

Affirming God's gift of life

20. It is now even more necessary than before to call for a fundamental re-shaping of the economic system and to affirm God's gift of life that is threatened in so many ways. Sustainable development, a concept prominent in international fora, still leaves powerful forces of globalization in command and does not question the underlying paradigm of continuous and unlimited progress and growth. Affirming God's gift of life to all creation in the midst of the pain, suffering, and destruction caused by economic globalization, it is imperative to discern a life-centred vision.

21. Jesus came so that all may have life and have it more abundantly (John 10:10). God's salvation in Jesus Christ not only means fullness of life for the human community, but the restoration of all creation to its goodness and wholeness. God's Holy Spirit comes to renew the whole creation. According to the creation stories of the Bible, the earth was meant to be home for all living creatures, which live in different spaces, but linked to each other in a web of relationships. The human community is placed within the wider community of the earth, which is embedded in God's household of life. It is this vision of a truly ecumenical earth, that challenges the ecumenical movement to search for new ways of revitalizing and protecting the communities of Indigenous Peoples and of the marginalized and excluded, participate in resistance against the growing domination of economic globalization, and engage itself in the building of a culture of peace and just relationships, a culture of sharing and solidarity.

22. Peoples' stories show and reflect the longing and desire for sustenance of life through fulfilling the essential needs of all people, for the protection of life through peace-building and peace making in situations of violence and war, for the enhancement of life through the strengthening of accountability in a truly democratic society and the improving of people's economic welfare by broadening opportunities and solidarity linkages, and for the enrichment of life through the deepening of people's spirituality and cultural activities as well as the up-building of just and sustainable communities.

23. Four essentials for a life-centred vision need to be nurtured: participation as the optimal inclusion of all involved at all levels, equity as basic fairness that also extends to other life forms, accountability as the structuring of responsibility towards one another and Earth itself, and sufficiency as the commitment to meet basic needs of all life possible and develop a quality of life that includes bread for all but is more than bread alone.

The task of the ecumenical family

24. What should be the response of the churches in the face of this challenge? What is the task of the ecumenical family? What should be the role of the churches through the World Council of Churches? How should churches and the WCC relate to others who struggle to understand and meet the challenges posed by globalization? How can we be vehicles of God's jubilee so central to Jesus' message (Luke 7:18-23)? That response must be named by each person and community represented here.

25. We acknowledge that in the context of globalization we have compromised our own convictions. We repent for the ways the power of new technologies, the lure of having things, the temptations to superiority and power have diverted our attention from our neighbour who suffers. We acknowledge the temptation we have to strive for our own inclusion in a world which has space for a privileged few. Lest our confession and repentance be hollow, we are called to discover and restore our solidarity with the excluded ones.

26. It is the task of the WCC to strengthen the ecumenical dimension in the life of the churches and provide space necessary for dialogue and mutual up-building towards a common witness by the churches locally, regionally and internationally. There is a need to strengthen the voice and representation by the WCC on international levels, a representation that can build on the capacity to analyze global trends, but one also that depends upon the kind of networking, support and transformation the WCC can muster as the churches own instrument. Critical to the vision of earth as home is the call for people in very different situations and contexts to practice faith in solidarity and affirm life on earth together.

27. In retrospect, it is clear that since the seventh assembly in Canberra the different programmatic areas of the WCC have been increasingly aware of the challenges and dangers inherent in the process of globalization. The new central committee and all of the member churches should be encouraged to develop a more coherent approach to the challenges of globalization, with a focus on life in dignity in just and sustainable communities.

Recent WCC publications on globalization and economic matters

1. Tony Addy (ed), *The Globalizing Economy: New Risks-New Challenges-New Alliances*, WCC-Unit III: Geneva, 1998
2. Tony Addy (ed), *The Globalizing Economy: New Risks-New Challenges-New Alliances*. Summary of Recommendations, WCC-Unit III: Geneva, 1998
3. Bas de Gaay Fortman/Berma Klein Goldewijk, *God and the Goods: Global Economy in a Civilizational Perspective*, WCC: Geneva, 1998
4. Richard Dickinson. *Economic Globalization: Deepening Challenge for Christians*, WCC-Unit III, Geneva, 1998
5. Rob van Drimmelen, *Faith in a Global Economy*, WCC: Geneva, 1998
6. Samuel Kobia, *The Changing Role of the State and the Challenge for Church Leadership in Africa*, in: Echoes 14, WCC-Unit III: Geneva, 1998, pp. 8-11
7. Julio de Santa Ana, *Sustainability and Globalization*, WCC: Geneva, 1998
8. WCC-Unit III (ed), Dossiers I and II on Multilateral Agreement on Investment, Geneva, 1998
9. WCC-Unit III (ed), Featuring Globalization, Echoes 12, Geneva, 1997

"Together on the Way, 5.3. Globalization"
Eighth Assembly, Harare, 1999.

Globalization is not simply an economic issue. It is a cultural, political, ethical and ecological issue. Increasingly, Christians and churches find themselves confronted by the new and deeply challenging aspects of globalization which vast numbers of people face, especially the poor. How do we live our faith in the context of globalization?

Recommendations (Adopted)

1. It is our deep conviction that the challenge of globalization should become a central emphasis of the work of the WCC, building upon many significant efforts of the World Council of Churches in the past. The vision behind globalization includes a competing vision to the Christian commitment to the oikoumene, the unity of humankind and the whole inhabited earth. This recognition should be reflected in our efforts to develop our Common Understanding and Vision as well

as in the related activities of member churches and other ecumenical bodies. Although globalization is an inescapable fact of life, we should not subject ourselves to the vision behind it, but strengthen our alternative ways towards visible unity in diversity, towards an oikoumene of faith and solidarity.

2. The logic of globalization needs to be challenged by an alternative way of life of community in diversity. Christians and churches should reflect on the challenge of globalization from a faith perspective and therefore resist the unilateral domination of economic and cultural globalization. The search for alternative options to the present economic system and the realization of effective political limitations and corrections to the process of globalization and its implications are urgently needed.

3. We express our appreciation of the call by the World Alliance of Reformed Churches' 23rd General Council (Debrecen, 1997) for a committed process of recognition, education and confession *(processus confessionis)* regarding economic injustice and ecological destruction and encourage the WCC member churches to join this process.

4. In view of the unaccountable power of transnational corporations and organizations who often operate around the world with impunity, we commit ourselves to working with others on creating effective institutions of global governance.

5. It is of high priority to improve the capacity of the WCC to respond to the challenge of globalization with a more coherent and comprehensive approach. This includes especially close co-operation and co-ordination of work on economic and ecological issues.

6. Work on globalization should build upon and strengthen existing initiatives of churches, ecumenical groups and social movements, support their cooperation, encourage them to take action, and form alliances with other partners in civil society working on issues pertinent to globalization as, particularly:

- formulating alternative responses to the activities of transnational corporations, the Organization for Economic Cooperation and Development, the International Monetary Fund, the World Bank, the World Trade Organization, the International Labour Office and related multilateral agreements in order to identify the harmful as well as positive impact of their policies in a competent manner;
- advocating and campaigning for the cancellation of debt and a new ethics and system of lending and borrowing;

- cooperating with initiatives for a new financial system including a tax on financial transactions (Tobin tax) that can be used to support the development of alternative options, limits to the unregulated flow of capital, etc.;
- supporting initiatives to address unemployment and the deteriorating conditions of work faced by workers in all regions as a result of globalization;
- enabling and supporting local alternatives through new forms of organizing production, fair trade, alternative banking systems and, particularly in highly industrialized countries, changes in life-style and consumption patterns;
- reviewing the churches' own dealing with land, labour, unemployment and finances as, for example, the ethical investment of pension funds and other financial resources, the use of agricultural land, etc.;
- promoting economic literacy and leadership training on globalization and related issues;
- reflecting on economic issues as a matter of faith.

SELECTED BIBLIOGRAPHY

Addy, Tony. *The Globalising Economy: New Risks – New Challenges – New Alliances*. Geneva: World Council of Churches Publications, 1998.

Batista, Israel, ed. "Social Movements: A Personal Testimony." *Social Movements: Challenges and Perspectives*. Geneva: WCC Publications, 1997.

Chomsky, Noam. *Profit Over People: Neoliberalism and the Global Order*. New York: Seven Stories Press, 1999.

Cone, James H. "Whose Earth is it Anyway?" in Hessel, Dieter, and Larry Rasmussen, eds. *Earth Habitat: Eco-Justice and the Church's Response*. Minneapolis, MN: Fortress Press, 2001.

Cone, James H. "Whose Earth is it Anyway?" Risks of Faith: *The Emergence of a Black Theology of Liberation*, 1968-1998. Boston: Beacon Press, 1999.

Dickinson, Richard. *Economic Globalization:: Deepening Challenge for Christians*. Geneva: WCC Publications, 1998.

Kahl, Brigitta. "Fratricide and Ecocide: Genesis 2-4." In *Working on Theology of Life: A Dossier*. Geneva: WCC Unit III, 1998.

Orteza, Edna. "The Sokoni, A Story." In *Working on Theology of Life: A Dossier*. Geneva: WCC Unit III, 1998.

Rasmussen, Larry. *Earth Community, Earth Ethics*. Maryknoll, NY: Orbis Books, 1996.

_____. "Sustainable Development and Sustainable Community: Divergent Paths." *Development Assessed: Ecumenical Reflections and Actions on Development*. Geneva: WCC Publications, 1995.

_____. "Theology of Life and Ecumenical Ethics." In *Working on Theology of Life: A Dossier*. Geneva: WCC Unit III, 1998.

Robra, Martin. "Theology of Life Consultation at Union Theological Seminary." In *Working on Theology of Life: A Dossier*. Geneva: WCC Unit III, 1998.

Ronfeldt, David, John Arquilla, Graham E. Fuller, and Melissa Fuller. *The Zapatista Social Netwar in Mexico*. Santa Monica, CA: Rand, 1998.

de Santa Ana, Julio, ed. *Sustainability and Globalization*. Geneva: WCC Publications, 1998.

Shiva, Vandana. *Biopiracy: The Plunder of Nature and Knowledge*. Boston: South End Press, 1997.

Van Eldren, Martin, and Rob Van Drimmelen, eds. "Work in a Sustainable Society." *Ecumenical Review*, 48:269-391, July 1996.

Visser 't Hooft Endowment Fund for Leadership Development. *Sustainable Growth – A Contradiction in Terms: Economy, Ecology and Ethics After the Earth Summit*. Geneva: The Visser 't Hooft Endowment Fund for Leadership Development, 1993.

World Council of Churches. *Accelerated Climate Change: Sign of Peril, Test of Faith*. Geneva: World Council of Churches Publications, 1994.

_____. *Climate Change and the Quest for Sustainable Societies*. Geneva: WCC Publications, 1998.

_____. *Now is the Time: The Final Document and Other Texts from the World Convocation on Justice, Peace and the Integrity of Creation, Seoul, Republic of Korea, 5-12 March 1990*. Geneva: WCC Publications, 1990.

_____. *Report of the World Council of Churches' and the Lutheran World Federation's Delegation to the Third Session of the United Nations' Commission on Sustainable Development*. Geneva: WCC Publications, 1995.

_____. *Report to the WCC Member Churches Concerning the UN Earth Summit +5 Review Process*, 1997.

_____. *Searching for a New Heaven and a New Earth: An Ecumenical Response to UNCED*. Geneva, WCC Publications, 1992.